THE

21st-Century
Classroom

THE

21st-Century
Classroom

GABRIEL RSHAID

LEAD+
LEARN
PRESS

ENGLEWOOD, COLORADO

The Leadership and Learning Center
317 Inverness Way South, Suite 150
Englewood, Colorado 80112
Phone 1.866.399.6019 | Fax 303.504.9417
www.leadandlearn.com

Published by Lead + Learn Press, a division of Houghton Mifflin Harcourt.

Library of Congress Cataloging-in-Publication Data

Rshaid, Gabriel.
    The 21st-century classroom / Gabriel Rshaid.
        pages   cm
    Includes bibliographical references and index.
    ISBN 978-1-935588-49-8 (alk. paper)
    1. Education—Forecasting. 2. Educational change. 3. Continuing
    education. 4. Education—Effect of technological innovations on.   I. Title.
    LB41.5.R74 2013
    370—dc23
                                                                              2013033476

ISBN 978-1-935588-49-8

Manufactured in the United States of America

18 17 16 15 14   01 02 03 04 05 06

This book is dedicated to Ines, Belen, and Juan Pablo
(in order of appearance), who give meaning to my life
and have been so unbelievably selfless
in letting me embark on my learning journey,
despite the time it takes away from family life;
and to the memory of my parents,
who invested more than they could afford
on my education.

CONTENTS

ACKNOWLEDGMENTS

I would like to thank The Leadership and Learning Center for this new opportunity to reach out to a broader audience, Jessica Engman in the publications team for her constant support and help, and Alan Bernhard and the team at Boulder Bookworks for the most wonderful and efficient editing process ever. This book would not have been possible without the generous support and vision of the governance team at St. Andrew's Scots School, as well as what I was able to learn from my colleagues and friends at the school and, very especially, my students, from whom I have also learned so much and who have, even if unbeknownst to them, been instrumental in trying to see, through their eyes, what the future of education might look like. Last, and certainly not least, my big thanks to Sofia Sengenberger without whose wisdom and uncanny ability to always make things easier I would not have been able to even try to balance my hectic workload.

INTRODUCTION

It is not often that an author deliberately chooses for the title of a book a phrase that some would call an oxymoron. But I think the title *The 21st-Century Classroom* embodies much of what is so contradictory about our current approach to tackling this century's challenge to educators, and yet, it also conveys the hope that efforts can truly capitalize on the promise of 21st-century education.

The clear underlying paradigm of 21st-century education is lifelong learning. Generalized access to the Internet has not only minimized the importance of physical proximity but also granted access to all accumulated human knowledge. New content is being generated at a breathtaking pace and the ageless "sage on the stage" model that teachers have perpetuated as the default pedagogy has become increasingly and irreparably flawed.

Even the whole idea of the classroom is outdated. The word "classroom" owes its origin to the word "class"; its meaning can be traced back to the 17th century when it was used to refer to "a form or lecture reserved to scholars who had attained a certain level." The connotations of the word have transcended its etymology: now it bespeaks implicitly of a confined space and time during which lessons are given, mostly in the form of teachers lecturing and students passively absorbing knowledge.

Nothing can be further from the desired 21st-century paradigm, because today anybody can learn anything at any time, and knowledge (in itself a term that needs redefining) is just a few keystrokes away. Learning is no longer restricted to the confines of the classroom, or even to the school schedule. We can all truly become lifelong learners; lifelong learning, a term that hitherto has featured prominently in empty clichés in countless school mission statements, can now finally be for real.

The teacher's role has also changed fundamentally. Within the traditional fixed-content model, the teacher was absolutely indispensable for learning, being the essential conduit to pass on knowledge. Thomas and Seely Brown (2011) state this with great clarity:

> For most of the twentieth century our educational system has been built on the assumption that teaching is necessary for learning to occur. Accordingly, education has been seen as a process of transferring information from a higher authority (the teacher) down to the student. This model, however, just can't keep up with the rapid rate of change in the twenty-first century. It's time to shift our thinking from the old model of teaching to a new model of learning.

Moving from a role of transmitting knowledge to one of mentor and facilitator, from a focus on passing on the learning to a focus on helping students acquire the skills to learn on their own, is much deeper than just a change in the job description. The proposed shift goes straight to teachers' hearts, and may very well gnaw at some of the reasons that made teachers choose the profession in the first place. Many teachers now active in schools opted to be educators because they truly love, mostly in a selfless way, to take their students to great heights by virtue of their lecturing, their explanations, and their ability to pour out a vast amount of knowledge so as to fill the vessels in their students' minds.

Today's fertile environment in which all knowledge is infinitely available exposes all of us in terms of our own relationship with learning. If we are learners at heart, and have embraced this most noble profession through our love of learning, the "stepping aside" that is required in our changed roles as 21st-century educators is not too unsettling, since we are passionate about sharing today's treasure trove of learning with our students. If, however, we enjoy teaching because of the superiority that stems from our expert knowledge, or the power that is automatically vested in any teacher that steps into a classroom, or the thrill of authority and the prerogative to be judgmental toward our students, we are going to be in trouble: nobody can presume to know everything anymore and, on many issues, our students will be much more knowledgeable than we are.

Even the axiomatic and sacrosanct idea of knowledge in itself may be questionable. The limitless nature of the Internet is not conducive to the former idea of knowledge as unambiguous. In his provocatively titled book *Too Big to Know: Rethinking Knowledge Now That the Facts Aren't the Facts, Experts Are Everywhere, and the Smartest Person in the Room Is the Room* (2012), David Weinberger boldly addresses the issue of knowledge in the 21st century:

> The new way of knowing is just now becoming apparent. Although we can't yet know its adult form, some aspects are taking form. Networked knowledge is less certain but more human. Less settled but more transparent. Less reliable but more inclusive. Less consistent but far richer. It feels more natural because the old ideals of knowledge were never realistic, although it's taken the networking of our culture to get us to admit this.

This almost blasphemous suggestion that indisputable knowledge may no longer be an option is, however, increasingly intuitive within our end user experience of being exposed to an overwhelming amount of information.

Within this dynamic, fast-paced, and quite volatile context, the phrase "21st-century classroom" becomes intrinsically contradictory: in the 21st century, learning becomes ubiquitous in time and space, and not encapsulated within the classroom. The underlying assumption of the word "class"—understood as a place where the teacher lectures—is no longer current or effective. It is time to completely rethink the model.

The New 21st-Century Classroom

Although this phrase is vilified, it can still signify a beacon of hope. Very often, when I confront educators with the magnitude and scope of the change required—how we need to drastically reassess many of the sacred tenets of schooling—they express a feeling of despair. Even everyday constraints can seem insurmountable in the face of so many needed changes. The leap required to move from our old model of education to the new one seems so vast that it is not even worth attempting. Half-hearted efforts to fit an old model of teaching within a completely new paradigm can be frustrating and tiring. Not infrequently, moving to a pedagogy more suitable for the 21st century is implicitly or explicitly associated with onerous technology investments.

And yet there are limitless opportunities, even taking into account all the constraints and limitations under which teachers operate every day, to start creating this new 21st-century classroom, which can be gradually developed out of a renewed mindset and related pedagogy.

The proposed change is still somewhat daunting, for it requires that we strip off many of our preconceptions about teaching and learning, and that we are ready to challenge some of the most venerable axioms about education and schooling. But this same change is also very promising for our own personal development and spiritual health: the road ahead requires us to rediscover the learners inside ourselves, and to view education as what it irreversibly and thankfully has become: a joyful, limitless opportunity for learning. When viewed through the prism of learning, change stops looking threatening and gradually turns into a great opportunity for continuous learning.

Efforts at reforming schools are perpetual, ranging from an exacerbated obsession with test scores to adapting market rules and corporate gospel to the educational environment. Most of them have been grandiose and pompous, and, unfortunately, have resulted in the all-too-familiar scenario of artificially rigorous measurements that are later refuted by conflicting research-based findings on the hitherto celebrated gains and improved scores.

This book is dedicated to exploring ways in which we can build a 21st-century classroom and better prepare our students for the demands of a world of constant change, a world that is full of unprecedented promise. The proposed changes that form the basis for a 21st-century pedagogy are radical in their essence, but nonthreatening in their implementation. This low-profile and yet far-reaching attempt at reform seems to be the only possible way in which the unsung heroes of the educational revolution in the 21st century—the teachers—can silently break through the public relations machine, the shortsightedness intrinsic to politics, the exasperating futility of educational bureaucracies, and the need for compliance with the rules of the game.

The development of the 21st-century classroom is not a linear process, and there are no recipe-style prescriptive steps to achieving success. The suggestions in this book are principle-based, and are not very risky, because they are steps in the right direction. Nobody knows better what works at the classroom level than teachers, and any long-lasting approach to reform must empower educators to do as they see best within their own reality. This is the principle under which Finland has emerged to be the most admired country in terms of its educational system (Sahlberg, 2011), and the one that resonates with our deeply honed education instincts, which revolt when we are ministered to from the pulpit by educational "experts" who, in some cases, have not even set foot in a classroom.

Education (along with certain more disreputable contenders) can lay claim to being among the oldest professions in the world, and the masters that have transcended their eras all had in common the most distinguishable, and still current, trait of a good teacher: a love of learning. In her book *The Death and Life of the Great American School System: How Testing and Choice Are Undermining Education* (2010), a surprisingly candid account of the maladies of the American educational system, Diane Ravitch goes beyond the systemic analysis of educational systems to relay this most universal of all truths regarding learning: "Teachers must be well educated and know their subjects. To impart a love of learning, they should love learning and love teaching what they know."

Most often, those of us who are parents can cut across all boundaries of political correctness and professional decorum when thinking about our own kids. If somebody granted me a single wish for my own children regarding their formal education, I would have no hesitation: that whatever they do in school, they are inspired to love learning. Beyond the strategies, ideas, thoughts, and reflections that I will lay out in the following pages, it is my hope that this book can serve to inspire educators to rediscover this most fundamental quality of our mission, not only as a fulfilling experience in itself, but also as the single most important trait for educational success and effectiveness in this puzzling but incomparably promising knowledge era.

CHAPTER ONE

The Challenge

In the space of a few years, and almost unintentionally, every rule in the educational game was changed, so much so that we could even say that it became "a whole new ball game."

Before the creation and ensuing massive development of the Internet, teachers operated in a model of scarcity, as economists are fond of referencing when framing the fundamental principles of economics. Because knowledge was limited and almost fixed in time, the teacher was an absolutely indispensable link between students and learning. Teachers were assisted by that most formidable of tools, the textbook, and were absolutely in control of how, what, and when learning occurred.

This paradigm for learning had an obvious impact on who chose to become a teacher. The teaching profession was attractive to those of us who thoroughly enjoyed passing on knowledge; it drew people who derived satisfaction from being able to transmit their learning to students. The "total control" dimension was also appealing to some teachers, even though they might not have been consciously aware of it. Teachers who stepped into a classroom were automatically invested with authority, which was derived not only from their indisputably superior knowledge but also from their absolute power over the instructional process.

The fixed model of knowledge was the origin of some of the very familiar characteristics of schools in the pre-Internet era: a heavily grades-based culture, assessments as rigid evaluations that focused mainly on content and factual recall, and a testing system in which there were right or wrong answers most of the time and, as a consequence, in which mistakes were not only discouraged but also penalized to the point that students felt stigmatized by the ghost of failure.

Because learning was so heavily dependent upon the teacher's knowledge, student achievement was inevitably shaped to the teacher's self-image. Assignments and evaluations often just targeted singular dimensions of learning, more often than not those that reflected mastery of the content, ability to solve true-or-false questions, or the skills traditionally honed over the years conforming to standards. Every student learned in the same way, and was expected to perform similarly and to the same level, and, even more aggravatingly, at the time specified in the fixed, one-chance-only, hallowed, sit-down written test.

Time was a particularly despotic dimension of learning. Deadlines were regarded as absolutes, and mastery needed to be acquired not as an objective for life, but rather for the time of the evaluation.

A heavy reliance on standardized testing as the prime measure of accountability resulted in an even more exacerbated focus on testing as the one and only measure of school success, with endless negative consequences regarding the self-esteem of students, teachers, and even whole school systems, which were subjected to impossible pressure under the auspices of the ill-fated No Child Left Behind Act, resulting in school closures and ruined careers.

The 21st-Century Challenge to Schools

The use of all those past-tense verbs throughout the preceding paragraphs hinted that these practices are outdated, but, unfortunately, this use of the past tense is mostly an exercise in wishful thinking, since many of the characteristics previously outlined still constitute the prevalent pedagogy currently in place in schools.

In his book *Why School? How Education Must Change When Learning and Information Are Everywhere* (2012), Will Richardson provides a harsh reality check:

Right now, though, based on visits to hundreds of schools in the past few years, I'd estimate that 95 percent of them are doing little or nothing to truly prepare their students for the world as it currently exists. Connecting and learning with other people online, distinguishing good information from bad, creating and sharing important works with the world: None of that (and a whole bunch of other stuff I could mention) is on the test. And sadly, therefore, we don't value it. It finds no place in our classrooms.

What we can euphemistically call the 21st-century challenge to schools is, undoubtedly, quite a daunting prospect, and one that has multiple dimensions. The changes required are not just changes in the way things are done, but fundamental shifts in many of the most basic tenets of curriculum design and—even more of an effort—fundamental changes in the way that curriculum is delivered by teachers.

Attempting to come up with a laundry list of the changes required is an effort that is almost self-contradictory, since the 21st-century environment is defined by constant instability and fast-paced change. However, some of the core principles of 21st-century education that have resulted in this completely new paradigm are one-way changes—irreversible in their nature. Therefore, it is useful to map out some of the main drivers for educational change that provide a glimpse of the magnitude and scope of the modifications required.

From Learning Curriculum to Lifelong Learning

In the fixed-knowledge model, where all chances to learn were extinguished the moment the students stepped out of the school gate until they entered other formal learning institutions, carefully defining a prescribed curriculum was fundamentally important. In effect, in the paradigm where students were vessels to be filled with knowledge, carefully selecting what to pour into those vessels, which, metaphorically, would be sealed off until a further chance to engage in formal studies occurred, was obviously a top priority. Curriculum discussions were the centerpiece of many of the most important deliberations happening within the school environment, and the ensuing focus on how to assess the learning of the curriculum led to the endless issues regarding standards, standardized testing, school improvement, test scores, and the litany of pronouncements by educational bureaucracies that have plagued schools in recent memory.

Richardson (2012) provides an apt metaphor to illustrate the old model of scarce knowledge and how it becomes almost absurdly flawed in the current context of infinitely available information:

> Imagine walking into a huge library, sitting down at a work table in the middle, and waiting for someone to bring you only the materials they consider important reading. Despite the library's hundreds of thousands of books and magazines and journals and recordings, you just get to read (and perhaps learn from) a very, very, very small segment of those—the same tiny segment everyone else who visits the library gets to read and learn from. All the rest sits quietly in the stacks, untouched. Now imagine how large the library would be that we'd have to build if we only stocked the materials included in the typical K–12 curriculum. You get the idea. At a time when content and teachers were scarce, it made sense to want our kids to be "learned." If all they had was limited access to a relatively small stockpile of knowledge and information, we'd need to cram all that stuff in, just in case they might need it one day. And we'd better have adults who could "teach" that material and test for its mastery.

Within the 21st-century environment of ubiquitous, continuous learning that can occur regardless of time, space, and the previously essential intervention of a teacher, the prime objective of schools moves from helping students accumulate content and learn a fixed curriculum to helping students acquire the skills needed to learn throughout life, and even more important and more difficult, igniting in students the desire to learn for life.

Whereas the main objective of school systems used to be quantifiable and standardized, the real needed focus of formal instruction now is more holistic and hazy, and, as such, is very much a challenge to school systems that have not been designed to aim for a high-level objective that cannot be broken into a linear sequence of carefully constructed steps.

Like most of the changes needed, this first—and essential—dimension of the challenge requires a shift in mindset, and it requires letting go of traditional built-in preconceptions about what constitutes a rigorous curriculum and what a school that accomplishes academic excellence looks like. It also entails having the strength to defy current external expectations, which use numeric measurements as the de facto yardstick to gauge the quality of a school.

Moving to a model of lifelong learning from a model of just complying with external one-size-fits-all standards is, without a doubt, the right thing to do, and is a strong ethical imperative, but it is still a tall order. This far-reaching objective can only be accomplished over an extended period of time, because it requires much more than just a change in methods or even in pedagogy. Such a fundamental transformation involves a great deal of soul searching, as well as the patience to see these changes come to fruition and the drive to see them through despite the many constraints and pressures faced by school administrators.

From Teaching to Learning

The "teaching and learning process" is one of the many interchangeable phrases authors and experts use to attempt to describe what is going on in schools. The really interesting undertone to the expression is that, in the pre-Internet era, there were heavily asymmetrical connotations associated with it.

In effect, when the teacher was the sole master of learning, the balance was clearly tipped in favor of the teaching dimension of the process. The mere thought of the innumerable pedagogical trends, schools of thought, and ephemeral flavor-of-the-moment pedagogical fads that any of us who have been long enough in schools have gone through attests to the fact that they are directed to teaching and not necessarily, or maybe only indirectly, to learning.

Most of the well-intentioned efforts to submit classroom educators to re-education have been almost entirely focused on teaching—on the utmost goal of becoming better teachers, improving teaching techniques, and refining the art of conveying knowledge. However, even though the importance of enhancing the instructional process from the "giving" end cannot be denied, the change in some of the basic axioms in education brought forth by the knowledge era, and the need to refocus school efforts toward lifelong learning, require that we also acknowledge the importance of enhancing the instructional process from the "receiving" end—the learning part of teaching and learning.

Schools need to center their efforts more on the learning side of the equation. Recently, especially with the nascent but powerful and very promising applications of neuroscience to classroom practice, there is a growing trend to think more about learning, but a comprehensive and extensive body of research needs to be gradually developed to target how to improve student learning, and, equally important, to venture into the more murky realm of how to improve students' motivation and intrinsic desire to learn, which are quintessential to lifelong learning.

This evolutionary model for schools is not just a cosmetic change of roles or rewriting of teachers' job descriptions. The changes that need to be made gnaw deeply at some of the very reasons why teachers chose the profession in the first place, and entail not just a relearning of the trade but also a profound re-examination of our own relationship with learning and how we can become colearners with our students. At the end of the day, this is the only authentic way to ensure educational success in this new environment.

In his manifesto for educational change, Will Richardson (2012) spells out the need for a transformative approach to our role: "There should also be no doubt that, to prepare students to be learners, we need adults in classrooms who can serve as outstanding role models for learning. If we're to develop learners who can make sense of the whole library, we must already be able to do that ourselves. In other words, the adults in the room need to be learners first and teachers second."

For a school to change from a place where teachers teach and students learn to a place where everybody learns, a school-wide commitment to modeling the learner mindset is essential. The transformation should permeate all layers of the organization, including school and district leadership, and it is important to relinquish the demand to see results immediately after professional development efforts. The difference between espousing a learning mindset and learning the latest tools of the trade is that with a learning mindset, results will become self-evident only after an extended period of time, and it will be almost impossible to measure the effect utilizing conventional educational parameters of success.

From Contents to Skills

Another transformational shift has to do with the almost obvious need to gradually move away from a curriculum based on memorizing content and assessments that target factual recall to a curriculum that fosters the development of skills and assessments that measure the attainment of those skills. The traditional approach to designing a curriculum was to structure delivery of lessons around the core disciplines (mostly literacy and numeracy, followed by science and social sciences) and then to sequence contents to ensure that students emerged from formal schooling with a solid knowledge base that would serve them well in the world of limited knowledge.

In the world of nearly infinite information accessible at our fingertips, it is no longer so relevant to acquire and remember so much content; rather, students need to have the skills they need to learn, and—I cannot stress this enough—students need curiosity and the desire to learn.

In his "Hole-in-the-Wall" experiments, well-known researcher Sugata Mitra made computers accessible to poor, illiterate children living in slums in India as a way to demonstrate that when children want to learn, they can do so despite seemingly insurmountable challenges, such as not knowing English, or having no prior computer instruction. In his e-book *Beyond the Hole in the Wall: Discover the Power of Self-Organized Learning* (2012), a synthesis of his multi-year research on self-learning, Mitra takes a clear stand on this issue: "What kids know is just not important in comparison with whether they can think. Learning math and spelling is far less important than learning the act of learning."

This conversion of the schooling model from a focus on contents to a focus on skills constitutes a formidable challenge, since schools and educators everywhere have evolved over time to develop carefully honed reflexes and instincts that are all geared toward the learning of content. Teachers intuitively think that a system more geared toward skills undermines content rigor, and they will push back against any curriculum that they think lacks rigor in terms of content that needs to be remembered.

Having said this, however, we also need to acknowledge that a school curriculum cannot be structured purely on the development of skills with no care given to learning content. Students should not walk about all their lives as empty vessels, as if they were computers whose contents are switched off the moment they lose Internet connectivity. The million-dollar question in this matter, and one that seldom gets asked, is how much baseline content is necessary, and for what purpose? How much content and from what disciplines do students need to know in order to have a solid base upon which to build higher-order knowledge and 21st-century skills, and to be cultured individuals who can function in an environment in which they are not constantly connected to the Internet?

When planning curriculum, the foremost consideration is traditionally given to content. Once again, the needed learning outcomes are determined in terms of the traditional disciplines and contents structured and sequenced, with spiraling of content and, hopefully, with alignment policies that eliminate repetition and account for any holes in the content learned. Such are the well-intentioned curriculum efforts that have taken place in schools since time immemorial. The skills gained through the mastering of content were almost an afterthought.

When it becomes paramount that students learn certain skills (i.e., 21st-century skills), the traditional curriculum design thought process, which places emphasis on content, should be inverted; that is, the desired skills should be listed and prioritized, and then the subjects and content that best suit the development of each skill should be chosen in order to catalyze the learning of that skill. Other than that elusive, yet-to-be-determined basic content threshold that all students should access as part of their core cultural learning, subjects and disciplines should be selected based on how well they promote the learning of the skill and not the reverse.

From Learning within Fixed-Time and Fixed-Content Standards to Learning in Itself

Another profound and far-reaching transformation that is needed is related to the core business at schools—learning. The postindustrial model of school, with its welcome massive reach of education that extended to so many more people, slowly evolved into a model that became heavily fixed in its outcomes and standardized in terms of the learning to be acquired by students throughout their time in school.

In the fixed model of knowledge, where certain content had to be mastered, a one-size-fits-all education model made more sense. Students had to conform to what their teachers thought constituted learning, and the educators in turn based their learning requirements on standards mandated for them by whatever current accountability framework was in place.

To further emphasize this tunnel vision focused on what were considered to be adequate learning outcomes, assessments more often than not came in one form and were fixed in time, adding an impending threat that struggling students quickly came to dread: learning had to occur by the date of the evaluation in order for the students to get credit and retain their self-esteem. It was not acceptable for learning to happen significantly before or—God forbid—after the assessment. Students were expected to perform to a rigorous time frame unless they were branded with special considerations.

Retests were not the norm, and most of the time students were subjected to a narrowly defined set of expectations that had to be conformed to by a given date and within a certain amount of time with no further chances, in a do-or-die environment that, paradoxically, was far more stringent than all but a handful of real-life situations. (The exceptions—brain surgeons and test pilots, for example—would not be expected to operate under trial-and-error conditions, but they learn and are assessed through simulations, the quintessential trial-and-error environment.) Any concessions for students who fell out of the carefully defined assessment time frame had demeaning connotations: students took "remedial" tests, implying that students who needed a second chance were ill or somehow incompetent, or attended summer school or other last-ditch attempts at gaining credit so as not to fall off the educational ladder. Those concessions undermined irreversibly that most precious and fragile of human traits—self-esteem, which is especially vulnerable in young children.

The aforementioned blatant and self-evident disconnects from what we know to be true about effective education, however, were not brought forth by the collective ill intentions of countless educators conspiring to make the lives of children miserable and turn school into a painful experience. The model came about as a logical result of external societal demands to conform to fixed outcomes for success, a knowledge paradigm that sought vainly to encompass all existing knowledge and reduce it to sets of quantifiable indicators, and a general drive for material wealth as a worthy goal, as opposed to the now, thankfully, more prevalent goal of seeking personal realization and higher purpose. The intention of the traditional school system was to make students knowledgeable through rigor, and it operated on the premise that a world with rewards and punishments did not have any need for intrinsic motivation. The axiom was that, unless a rigorous framework was in place, some students would "beat the system" and escape without the minimum required content mastery.

Now we are witnesses to the painful cultural clash caused by two "new" ideas: the 21st-century realization that the carrots-and-sticks model does not work, and a sort of digital renaissance that acknowledges that every student can and must learn, and that if we cater to each student's learning abilities and cognitive style, every student will be able to achieve significant learning. From Howard Gardner's theory of multiple intelligences (2006) to the latest neuroscience findings, new information about how learning happens is causing educators to do away with the traditional and increasingly ineffective model of education and develop a new pedagogy that focuses on the learning itself rather than on meeting external demands and complying with fixed expectations.

Until external demands are more in line with what educators have always known to be right—a more humane approach to learning that is not judgmental—teachers and administrators will continue to have to deal with a fair amount of external pressure in terms of what needs to be done at school. But even within existing constraints, a pedagogy that focuses more on learning than on complying with fixed parameters can be deployed. The goal is to remain true to the universal primary objective of schools—learning—while providing a more personalized curriculum that is tailored to students' needs and is not as rigid as the current prevalent school models.

From Learning in the Classroom to Ubiquitous Learning

A major game changer as a consequence of widespread access to the Internet through mobile devices is that information is literally just a few keystrokes away. In the ages-old classroom-based model, the moment the bell rang freeing students of what was usually associated with tedium marked a clear boundary for learning, but schools now have to deal with a much richer scenario of infinitely available knowledge that is accessible regardless of location thanks to the increased sophistication and connectivity of miniaturized devices.

These gigantic forward leaps in accessibility only legitimized what educators had been whispering about forever: that there is as much value in extracurricular activities, field trips, sports, drama, and music as in formal academic instruction within the classroom. Whenever people reflect back on their school years, they almost always highlight some of the things that happened outside of the classroom as being their most formative and memorable learning experiences.

In the relatively disconnected world that existed before the Internet, any activities that took place outside the classroom were automatically disassociated from learning, given the physical impossibility of carrying a body of knowledge outside of the formal learning environment of the classroom. Nowadays, within our hyper-connected world, access to learning is seamless and can accompany any educational activity almost regardless of space and time.

Part of the transformation that is required entails acknowledging that learning does not only occur in the classroom: that the informal spaces that many modern-day school designs are already incorporating can serve to host equally productive informal learning activities, and that any form of extracurricular activity can be connected into learning with the use of a cell phone.

Clearly, this massive extension of learning poses a dire challenge to teachers, whose intrinsic authority emanates from being the possessors of knowledge and from holding court in the classroom. Extending learning beyond the confines of the classroom literally takes teachers out of their comfort zone and, as such, needs to be carefully addressed when reassessing a 21st-century curriculum.

From Technology for Teaching to Technology for Learning

We have been saying that technology is on the verge of revolutionizing education for the last 30 years. However, regardless of any specific assessment of the effectiveness of the implementation of technology in education, it goes without saying that the efforts to make technology an everyday ally in education have fallen short of the mark, and have failed to deliver on the promise of providing students with a 21st-century education.

It is hard to identify a single culprit for this letdown, but the main reason why technology has not made more significant inroads into classrooms has to do with a myopic focus on the object of its implementation. In effect, most specialized education devices and technology programs touted by a myriad of vendors have targeted the teacher, and have aimed to enhance the instructional process.

This is a laudable goal, but many of these flawed attempts at technology integration missed out on the real promise of technology: to revolutionize not the way we teach, but the way we learn. From the early days of multimedia CDs that dazzled teachers with the promise of a handful of videos that actually showed things in motion instead of the fixed text of print encyclopedias and textbooks, to Smart Boards and document cameras, the push for technology served mostly to reinforce a teacher-centric model of education.

The most common use of technology in schools still involves the teacher lecturing and being the center of everything in the classroom, albeit with the inclusion of the use of a PowerPoint presentation to dole out the content of the lesson, on what constitutes a glorified, animated, and illuminated blackboard.

The paradigm shift required is far-reaching: instead of thinking of how technology can enhance teaching, we should be thinking about how technology can become a powerful catalyst for learning. Schools implementing 1:1 technology programs—that is, providing one laptop or other personal device for each student—is a well-known trend that has had varying results, but, being realistic, most schools cannot afford a full-fledged technology investment that provides one device per student. Even in schools that can, if the pedagogy is not changed in order to take advantage of unlimited access to information, it will not really constitute a dramatic change, or one that capitalizes on the implicit promise of using technology for learning.

The more recent BYOD (bring your own device) trend is far more realistic in terms of reaching more students, but creates a challenge of uniformity of access and tech capability for all students. However, regardless of the extent and magnitude of the technology investment, the overarching need is to shift the focus of technology programs from the teaching dimension toward a pedagogy that fully exploits the unlimited potential of technology for learning.

Many well-intentioned efforts have attempted to utilize the technology platform within the old pedagogy, such as the infamous on-screen marking programs, scanning evaluations for teachers to scribble notes on their computers, or the more commonly used standardized tests that have students ticking boxes for automatic marking. These attempts are only lukewarm: at best they embody more efficient methods for the old paradigm, and at worst some are so cumbersome to develop and implement that they inhibit schools from considering any further ideas.

The development of a pedagogy for learning using technology requires a more radical change in thinking; it requires taking a leap of one order of magnitude at least. It entails thinking in terms of games, applications of neuroscience to diagnose learning styles and tailor the learning experience to students, fully immersive three-dimensional realistic environments, expert systems, and other technological innovations that are yet to come.

Change in the School Setting

Even more daunting than the first question about what needs to be changed in order to develop a 21st-century curriculum is the next question: how can we actually effect change in schools?

Schools are, by nature, very conservative institutions, and the notions of many administrators about what is right in terms of education have remained almost immutable over the centuries. I once read somewhere that if Aristotle and Plato were to come back to life after thousands of years, the former would be at a loss to understand the current tools and techniques of the medical trade, whereas the latter, when it comes to learning, would have no trouble recognizing the venerable instructional model in use today for what it has always been.

The kind of change required is unsettling and quite contradictory to the nature of most people who have embraced the teaching profession. The new name of the game in schools would be to confidently embrace uncertainty, to look at change through the prism of learning, and to let go of the control long treasured by teachers in the pre-Internet era, when they were absolutely indispensable to learning.

Many of the proposed changes entail giving up not only on the idea of knowing everything, but also on one of the basic premises under which most curricula are designed—that students must conform to fixed outcomes and univocal standards for learning.

In the best cases, it was the teacher who designed assessments and drew out course requirements and expectations for students, mostly in the image of what learning looked like for the teacher. In another common but dreaded scenario, some external all-powerful authority determined what and how students should learn in the form of standards and standardized examinations.

It would be fruitless to go down the well-trodden path of discussing the pervasive evil of standardized examinations and fixed expectations—the one-size-fits-all scenario that is universally hated by teachers and stoically endured by students to the detriment, more often than not, of their self-esteem.

The point is that regardless of whether constraints and expectations are internal, from the teacher, or external, from stakeholders, changes need to take place despite these seemingly insurmountable constraints, even though demand for innovation is superficial at best. There is an awareness among educators of the need for change, and voices can be heard increasingly demanding that schools decisively enter the 21st century, but as of yet there has been no overwhelming push from the public or stakeholders to do so. It is a sort of catch-22 situation, where until we manage to capture people's imagination about the promise of 21st-century education, we will find it difficult to be innovative and meet external demands.

I involuntarily flinch every time I see a presentation or sales pitch about an educational program, product, or professional development offering when the presenter, after extolling the virtues of the program or product in question, delivers the coup de grace: "and test scores actually improve!" The hard truth is that developing and delivering a 21st-century curriculum will undoubtedly serve our students well and will provide them with the skills needed to become fully fledged citizens of the knowledge society, and that in the long run these improved skills will yield results, but there is no direct correlation between 21st-century educational innovation and performing better on the tests created within the old model of education.

How, then, can we implement change? There is much that can be done to advance the cause of 21st-century practices in the school setting even within existing conditions, and without the need for exorbitant investments. Even though the magnitude and scope of the change needed appears to be almost incompatible with the status quo, there are plenty of initiatives that can find their way to the classroom and gradually start shifting the mindset toward a very different conception of education.

Tackling the status quo head on is a losing proposition, and a futile one. It is more useful to start infusing 21st-century practices into our classrooms before the powers that be and the educational bureaucracies dictate that we do so. These small changes will come with little fanfare but, hopefully, long-lasting effect. The way to start a learning revolution is not to come up with grandiose plans about reforming school systems, but rather to convert the instructional process slowly but steadily toward the principles previously outlined.

Educational Research and Good Practice

Whole volumes could be—and have been—written on how to conduct educational research, and the related methodology constitutes a specialty in itself. But the really rich and controversial debate related to educational research has to do with the validity of such efforts, and whether studies that are conducted and that postulate conclusions from which teaching strategies are derived really can claim universal validity.

Research usually takes an extended period of time over which certain hypotheses are tried out and measured in terms of their effectiveness, in most cases using a control group—a similar group of students who have not been subjected to that particular method or strategy and, as such, serve as a valid neutral basis for comparison.

Objections to educational research are multiple, but the main objects of the scorn of many practitioners of the noble art of teaching have to do with the context of the studies and how replicable such experiences are, and the validity of the measurements, which most of the time consist of some form or other of standardized assessments that are questioned in terms of whether they indeed do measure what is being sought.

I will not take sides in this debate, but I do want to explicitly clarify the conditions under which the recommendations and the research in this book have been chosen to be applicable to educators in real-life contexts.

The most vilified aspect of educational research has to do with the fact that it seeks to tell teachers point blank what they should be doing and postulate what works and what doesn't in education. This is particularly irritating to teachers who find themselves confronted with the extrapolated conclusions of studies that they know are not necessarily applicable to their own school systems or classrooms.

The strategies, ideas, methods, exemplars, and suggested courses of action in this book are derived mostly from common sense and from a careful and detailed analysis of some irreversible trends in 21st-century education, and they focus on the process and not the outcome.

In all of these suggestions there is an explicit regard for context, since teachers do know better than anybody else what can work in their real-life classroom situations. In describing how to translate 21st-century educational principles into classroom practices, I am not prescribing a set of infallible steps that will yield a certain result, but rather a set of ideas and principles that, regardless of their short-term outcome, constitute the right direction to go to prepare students for the world they will have to live in and a future that is by definition uncertain. Exemplars of programs and classroom strategies that will be showcased are just that, specific embodiments of some of the 21st-century principles that have worked in the particular context in which they were implemented. They are intended as living proof that it is possible to start laying out the foundation for a true 21st-century curriculum, and, hopefully, some applicable ideas can be garnered from their analysis, but by no means are they presented as programs that will work irrespective of where and how they are put into practice.

Are these research-based strategies? Yes, in that they are based on many years of research, study, and practice in school systems from around the world, but not in the conventional use of the term.

It is impossible, and even contradictory to the 21st-century environment, to attempt to measure and isolate the effect of these strategies and ideas in ways that unequivocally demonstrate their effectiveness, as most conventional research practices dictate. In many cases, some of the processes that are suggested are intended to fill in gross gaps in our system by addressing some of the capabilities needed by students in the 21st century, and, as such, are valid and worthwhile in their mere proposition.

Thomas and Seely Brown (2011) come up with a great reference to one of the hitherto timeless principles about education, which illustrates the new environment we operate in:

> Many educators, for example, consider the principle underlying the adage, "Give a man a fish and feed him for a day, teach a man to fish and feed him for a lifetime," to represent the height of educational practice today. Yet it is hardly cutting edge. It assumes that there will always be an endless supply of fish to catch and that the techniques for catching them will last a lifetime.

It is not my intention to prescribe any condescending set of standard steps to teach you how to fish, but quite the opposite; I want to present ideas, thoughts, strategies, and even some specific examples, hoping that you will be able to make use of a few tips here and there, and knowing that it is you who will best discern what is applicable to your educational reality.

CHAPTER TWO

The Vision

"The only thing worse than being blind is having sight but no vision."

HELEN KELLER

There is a scene in one of the Indiana Jones movies that has, maybe unwittingly, far transcended the otherwise lighthearted adventure series. In *Indiana Jones and the Last Crusade*, Jones needs to cross a great chasm, and he has been given instructions that when he gets to the edge of the precipice, he just needs to take a step forward and a bridge will materialize. With great trepidation he does so, only to find that the bridge was there all along, camouflaged within the landscape and thus, until he stepped onto it, invisible to him.

Education is just one among many professions facing a similar scenario. The new, dazzling, interconnected world presents us with a wide void to cross, and no better option than our popular hero had—to plow ahead, hoping that a bridge will materialize under our feet. To make matters worse, for those of us in education, the main effect of the increasing availability of unlimited information and newly ubiquitous learning directly impacts our core business. As if that were not enough, the rest of the world is explicitly looking over our proverbial shoulders to take note of how we are preparing our students for the elusive and undefined future so that they can be productive in their chosen fields.

The reason that particular movie scene has captivated people's imaginations is that Indiana decides to take a leap of faith, metaphorically giving preeminence to the vision of where he must go over the anxiety caused by the chasm he must cross to bridge the gap. And the lesson learned is quite powerful, especially in turbulent times when we find that we are ill-equipped to go about our business in the conventional way. The lesson is that even when we are not very sure of what the tools, strategies, and new pedagogy might be, there is a great need to have a powerful vision that propels us forward and that helps us dare to take the plunge without such scrupulous regard for defining every step of the way across the abyss.

For it is, indeed, an abyss. The preceding chapter illustrated the magnitude of the change needed in education, but we must remember that the existence of such a wide gap between our current reality and our goals for the future should not paralyze us. Our current predicament and constraints do not make trying to bridge the gap a futile effort. The key to moving forward is to have a strong vision.

The Importance of the Vision

Organizations are having a hard time trying to adjust their usual ways of planning for the future. The venerable strategic plan approach, which consists of an extended discernment process involving multiple stakeholders in the organization usually led by an external facilitator whose job is to help them "see the light," is now hopelessly discredited, despite some die-hard attempts from more conservative leaders who still linger in the pre-Internet era of limited information and high predictability.

Massive strategic plan documents that attempt to forecast multi-year events, strategies, and related indicators are, during this time of dynamic instability, intrinsically flawed from their very conception. Douglas Reeves (2007) often makes reference to the quasi religion of "documentarianism," whose followers worshipped three-ring binders that never left the shelves, where they stood accumulating dust.

Schools have not escaped the reach of well-intentioned board members and other corporate leaders seeking to evangelize educators about the best corporate practices, and countless school leaders and administrators have been subjected to strenuous, sterile corporate exercises that even before our current uncertain times fell flat in the face of the field of education, which is so richly impossible to predict in that it deals with some of the deepest traits of human character.

Thankfully, common sense is slowly phasing out these practices, leaving us with the still pertinent question of how to plan for the future. Even though we cannot see what the future will look like or what jobs there will be and what skills will be needed, it is ever more important to define a clear vision for the road ahead.

When any attempt to establish a sequence of carefully laid out plans is deemed futile, working on a common vision for the future is even more important, because in the absence of specific recipes that add up to full organizational strategies, it is imperative that every member of the organization understands and internalizes the end goal, which will serve as a guide in uncertain times.

The importance of clear aspirational goals that serve to move people beyond the frustration they experience as a result of the disconnect between where we are now and where we want to be cannot be stressed enough. Having an inspiring vision can create deeper motivation, which is the only long-term insurance policy that will help an organization move forward.

Defining the Vision

How can we define a vision for education in the 21st century? Here once more we stumble on time-honored reflexes that make us attempt to define, frame, and even write out the problems we are facing. But the problems we are facing will always be more holistic than anything we can precisely define.

I once saw a cartoon in a presentation, and the image has forever stuck with me as one of the best ways to describe our quandary in the field of education: a mother and her young son are walking on a road, and the mother, exasperated, tells her son, "Stop asking when we will get there! How many times have I told you that we are nomads?"

It is certainly quite countercultural and somewhat disturbing to leave the secure waters of precisely defined objectives and outcomes to move into the murkier realm of confident uncertainty, but it is one of the most important and necessary changes to our mindset. We have finely honed instincts that urge us to try to come up with definitions for everything, but the dynamically unstable scenario of planning for education in a world that has changed so drastically calls out for focusing on principles and internal motivation rather than an analytical sequence of carefully planned logical steps. Attempting to define the 21st-century challenge is not only almost futile, but also an exercise that will diminish the richness of the challenge and its associated opportunities.

Southwest Airlines is a well-known success story in the airline industry. Despite the troublesome times that airlines have faced in recent years, which resulted in several of them filing for bankruptcy, Southwest Airlines has consistently posted positive earnings, even during the most troubled times. The "secret" of their success lies in the inspiring vision of their founder and former CEO, Herb Kelleher, a larger-than-life individual whose relentless efforts to make the airline's employees the main focus of its corporate strategy cascaded into efficiency and unparalleled customer service. Once, when prompted to define the vision of his company, Kelleher got fed up and retorted, "It's murder to dissect" (Sarkar, 2005). Likewise, any attempts at boiling down a 21st-century vision for education in a paragraph not only will be self-defeating, but also will limit the richness of the vision.

That does not mean that the vision cannot be communicated; instead it means that communication of the vision should not be accomplished via the usual top-down delivery method where leaders take the pulpit and ceremoniously unveil the stone-engraved new mission statement, but rather it should be transmitted as a series of ubiquitous and continuous actions where leaders take advantage of opportunities to make references to the salient elements of the vision in a way that not only highlights the vision but also embodies its main principles.

The beauty of the 21st-century scenario is that, despite the almost hopeless underlying complexity and uncertainty, the main drivers are quite simple and will not change: an emphasis on lifelong learning and intrinsic motivation to learn. All the rest, which will undoubtedly be vulnerable to changes, is not essential to the vision.

Professional Development and 21st-Century Education

If we accept the need for a compelling vision and accept the fact that the vision cannot easily be included within a finite set of documents, a relevant question emerges: how can we create a professional development program that targets empowering teachers to carry out a 21st-century vision?

Professional development in education has long been a rather elusive and controversial issue. Although well-intentioned efforts by leaders to educate and enlighten their staff members have always been met with a certain degree of skepticism in any profession, educators would probably be listed very high in a hypothetical ranking of cynical reactions to professional development intentions.

This may have to do with the fact that teaching has historically been a very individual profession, where educators literally closed the door to their classrooms and were masters of what transpired within, with a system of accountability that had traditionally been quite lax. As such, any efforts to tell a teacher what works best are likely to be met with a less-than-receptive attitude.

But it must also be stated, in fairness to educators, that it is not infrequent that some of these professional development courses created by professional consultants, or even by some renowned authors, are based on a very partial view of education, on a theory cooked up as if its results were as reproducible as a science experiment, and passed on to teachers as the new holy grail. These courses very often have a certain disregard for the intrinsically complex and unique nature of our trade, a disdain for the views of practitioners, and they are also often presented by lecturers who have seldom set foot in a classroom and experienced the hard realities of teaching.

The attempt to encapsulate and simplify educational reality into a series of recipe-style steps that seems to be the norm in most courses does not help. Any educator can easily conjure images of professional development courses that have been politely listened to but privately shredded to pieces in faculty conversations.

In this context, coming up with a viable paradigm for professional development related to 21st-century education seems to be quite a formidable challenge. There is a need to communicate a powerful vision in ways that are more implicit than explicit, a vision that changes not only the role but more fundamentally the mindset of teachers regarding what is expected of them, and that creates and develops a completely new pedagogy that targets the learning of new skills by students. It looks like an almost impossible proposition.

As always in the case of 21st-century education, there is no direct answer, but there are fail-safe ways to go about meeting the challenge, though they require a change in the mindset of administrators and educational leaders. It is essential to internalize that learning is beneficial for its own sake and not just in terms of its outcomes. If administrators want to entice their teachers to become 21st-century teachers, they must become 21st-century learners themselves, and must generate professional development processes that encourage the faculty to do the same. The first step in a 21st-century professional development program is for the leadership team to regularly engage in learning experiences themselves. Whatever form they deem most appropriate— attending conferences, creating a study group or learning retreat, or any other method—it is absolutely essential that leaders model learning behavior themselves. And the key to the success of such a program is to let go of our need for specific outcomes. Learning can cover a range of very diverse topics, and it does not necessarily have to be utilitarian in its approach. Most professional development programs have shared an obsession that content should be immediately applicable, and even though nobody can dispute the good intentions of such an objective, it has alienated many engaged teachers for the simple reason that education is a complex and unique business, and often the programs fell short of the mark.

A 21st-century professional development program should not disdain the learning of the tools of the trade, and the suggestions in this book do not preclude battle-tested pedagogical techniques that undoubtedly will continue to serve teachers well in any context. However, there should be an equal focus on a learning program that involves everybody in the organization, from the topmost leaders to the first-rung practitioners, in gaining awareness about the main drivers of education for the future and the essential tenets of 21st-century education.

Since the future of education lies in gradually converting educators' mindsets to align with the principles of a 21st-century education, which requires a deep and meaningful change, professional development programs should focus on inspiring leaders and teachers to perceive the promise and benefits of moving to a 21st-century education model, to understand the inherent moral imperative, and to trust that the traits of that model will eventually find their way into classroom practice.

The ages-old tenet of professional development that calls for changing our conduct prior to changing our beliefs (since these are so much more difficult to change), and that has led to adult learning efforts that prioritize the "sequence-of-steps-to-success" professional development model, needs to be inverted. Given the magnitude, depth, and extent of the change needed, it is imperative that beliefs be targeted first, for the needed changes require a commitment that is deep enough to sustain it despite the uncertainty and lack of explicit guidelines.

A learning program for adults may include discussing the new skills needed by both students and teachers, the principles of 21st-century education, the need to change our focus from teaching to learning, the emphasis on lifelong learning, and many other defining features of 21st-century education that might seem rather far-fetched but that gradually start working on the collective mindset of all involved as a first step toward helping teachers acquire traits that must eventually be learned by students in class.

Self-Study

Any learning program that targets 21st-century education must necessarily be a 21st-century learning experience itself. When trying to entice adults to change their teaching to a more independent learning-centered approach, one of the most common mistakes is that for whatever reason (the size of the audience, time constraints, lack of technology, etc.), the learning experience is still conducted as if it were happening in the pre-Internet era, with the presenter walking participants through slides and encouraging limited interactions between participants, of the type "Turn to the person next to you and..."

If we are truly serious about shifting mindset, we need to make the learning of 21st-century skills and the construction of a new curriculum and related pedagogy an immersive experience, including intensive participation from attendees, constructing conclusions from the expertise of people in the room, having norms that encourage participants to create an open learning environment that allows for social media interaction and access to the Internet, encouraging the introduction of dynamic, nonclosed content that benefits from resources supplied by the participants themselves, processing vast amounts of text via word clouds or other nonlinear representations, intense use of multimedia, and so on and so forth.

Creating a 21st-century environment that closely mirrors what the learning experience of the future is all about is not just beneficial in that it provides the learner with a taste of the prescribed medicine: it also paves the way for reflection about the effectiveness, advantages, and frustrations of such an environment, as well as providing participants with the opportunity to start understanding and closing the generational gap between adults trying to come out of their comfort zones and the young learners under their charge, who would seamlessly take to such a learning landscape. Reflecting on one's own learning is an integral part of the 21st-century learning experience, since that part of the learning process is quintessential to the ultimate goal of lifelong learning. Assessing the success and extent of each learning experience provides necessary checkpoints along the road of lifelong learning.

Developing a 21st-Century Vision

I have stressed repeatedly how important it is to develop a collective, shared vision to guide the implementation of 21st-century learning. This may seem like a daunting challenge, especially to those who have gone though the experience of developing mission statements and the like, since those efforts often prove quite exhausting and not too fruitful.

A 21st-century vision is not the same thing as a mission statement. It would be impossible to boil down such a complex, dynamic, and confusing scenario into a couple of sentences. And even if you could magically condense all that the 21st century can bring in terms of education, such a statement would need to be updated and revised continuously.

Developing a vision is not about synthesizing ideas but rather about attempting to bring down some of the lofty fundamental principles and tenets of the new paradigm to the reality of schools. It is about making good on the promise of the knowledge era to truly revolutionize the way we learn, in ways that will effect a long-lasting and sustainable change. The goal in trying to give substance to the mostly ethereal promise of positive change in education is to harness some of the principles and traits of 21st-century learning and bring them to life in our educational practices.

As such, the ensuing suggestions for activities that can help materialize the vision are rather unconventional, since they do not follow the linear sequence of content and subsequent mastery that is common in most adult learning. True to the principles of 21st-century education, the exercises and activities that are presented tend to tap into educators' collective knowledge and experience. Learning is no longer a top-down process of standing and delivering information to a passive audience.

Weinberger (2012) stresses even further the need to tap into the collective expertise of all participants in the learning experience:

> As knowledge becomes networked, the smartest person in the room isn't the person standing at the front lecturing us, and isn't the collective wisdom of those in the room. The smartest person in the room is the room itself: the network that joins the people and ideas in the room, and connects to those outside of it.

Making the learning experience a collective and participative endeavor is no longer just a desirable trait but rather an essential element in a 21st-century pedagogy. The construction of a 21st-century vision must in itself become a cooperative learning exercise, not only to make the vision a collective construct and not a vertically imposed state of mind, but also to model 21st-century learning. Going through the 21st-century learning process may do much more to educate staff members than even the best courses that tell educators what to do and how to do it.

The following is a list of exercises that I have used with groups large and small in very diverse settings, that can serve as catalysts to jump-start the implementation of a 21st-century curriculum by attempting to bring down some "blue sky" thinking processes and relate them to the everyday reality of a particular school or district. These are just suggestions, and this is not meant to be an exhaustive list of all ways to develop a vision. All of these activities require a positive and cooperative group of attendees, all of whom are willing to stretch their level of involvement to go beyond daily implementation and are interested in building this collective vision. Most of these activities also call for a healthy sense of humor, and some creativity and imagination.

For most of the suggested activities, participants in the exercise will be required to send in their thoughts, ideas, comments, and resources related to the topics in question. The goal is to be able to register them electronically for later processing and distribution to participants.

We will delve deeper into this tool of 21st-century pedagogy later on, and analyze the possibilities, advantages, and disadvantages of its use; its potential for truly delivering crowdsourcing knowledge; and how to best apply it in a classroom setting. For the time being, we will focus on each of the techniques in terms of how they can help consolidate divergent thought processes and catalyze reflections about the vision, without regard for the procedure. It will be implicit that in all cases participants will be able to send in their ideas via an ad-hoc interface, and that those ideas can, in turn, be prioritized, sorted out, or processed in the form of word clouds.

A 21st-Century Lounge

For the most part, all activities are interchangeable, and there is no prescribed order for the sequencing of them, but it is advisable to start with this longer exercise, which is designed to be a first immersion into 21st-century educational thinking.

When intending to have participants learn about 21st century education, there is no specific order of contents or logical sequence of concatenated concepts that will yield results. Rather, the principles of 21st-century learning are garnered through an increased and progressive level of awareness, a nonlinear learning process that targets multiple dimensions, including even the emotional aspect of change, an important driver in terms of internal motivation.

The goal is to expose participants to a variety of stimuli related to the 21st-century scenario. In a room or adjoining rooms large enough for everyone to be able to circulate freely for a period of approximately 45 minutes to an hour, participants, if possible in silence, will move between stations and either read a short text or watch a short video related to the theme. These texts and videos at the stations must be carefully chosen so as to present multiple points of view about the topic, and should not necessarily be technical in their development. Stations could range from a motivational video, to one of the many videos that abound on YouTube that provide statistics about the new habits of students, to information about students' consumption of media, to a presentation about the changes in the 21st century, to a reflection on the possibilities of education in the future, and even to opinions against 21st-century education.

Once participants go through a station, either electronically (ideally, so as not to have to retype anything) or by writing on a piece of paper next to the station, they should be encouraged to write a short tweet-like spontaneous reflection on what they have just read/watched, as a way to document their first immediate reactions and feelings when confronted with the topic. All of these reflections will then be utilized by the facilitator in a way (which will depend a lot on the number of people in the room) that will express the group's collective feeling regarding 21st-century education.

This is an important step in the process of capturing the vision, since the outcome of the exercise is twofold: first, participants will be exposed to an overarching series of stimuli that will be chosen so as to cause the most profound impression possible regarding the promise and challenge of 21st-century education, with the goal to start permeating their level of consciousness; second, this activity will result in the development of an initial internalization of the vision, a sort of first-step emotional translation by the protagonists themselves of how they, from their own subjective and collective views, can provide a foundation for the otherwise still quite distant promises associated with the future of education.

In the effort to try to gradually converge the thought process, it is also important for the facilitator to start a reflection process based on what the participants have expressed, so a plenary session lasting a few minutes should top off the activity and help bring a sense of completion to the experience. It is advised that all of the documents generated be kept and later collated in some form (a blog) so that the collection of records of the successive activities can form a road map for the emerging 21st-century vision.

Main Themes

A subsequent reflection in small groups challenges participants, after they have been exposed to the texts and videos in the lounge activity, to identify the main drivers for 21st-century education, in very general terms:

- What are the main drivers for 21st-century education?
- What general changes would be needed in the current educational system?
- What is the role of technology in bringing about change?

Burning the Ships

Another very powerful and sometimes extremely cathartic activity is based on a historic event that is a very applicable metaphor for the crossroads that all educators are currently facing.

In 1519, on the eve of what would be a deciding battle in the conquest of Mexico, the legend goes that Spanish conquistador Hernan

Cortés burnt all the ships in his flotilla in plain sight of his troops, so as to pass along an unequivocal message: there was only one way to go—forward—and no going back.

Educators in the 21st century find themselves at a similar juncture. The new world that Cortés set out to conquer offered almost unlimited riches and promise, and yet still seemed overwhelmingly complex and distant, uncertain in terms of the possibility of success. However, and this is the most important dimension of the message: there is no going back. Regardless of any value judgments that we may have as educators about whether all of these changes are actually beneficial or not, the impact of technology on individuals and society and the pace and trend of such impacts are irreversible.

We can long for the good old days when students did not excessively rely on technology, or were not constantly wired to their portable devices, but nonetheless, technology will continue to open up unprecedented opportunities for multimedia, networking, and seamless communication, and innovation is being driven by market and profits, not by what would be best for the collective enlightenment of humanity.

So reminiscing about the past will not forestall the future. Like Cortés, we have burned our proverbial ships. We can revel in the excitement of the new land, but before we set out to venture into the future, it is also a good idea to do away with thoughts of going back the way we came, and, in the process, to shed many of the characteristics of the old school that have resulted in constraints and frustration.

When analyzing the differences between the "old school" and "new school" in seminars, it invariably surfaces that what participants regard as "old school" is mostly associated with tedium, boredom, and other not very flattering terms. And there are always particular things in every district and school that educators would gladly get rid of as they open up the gates of the future, and that they would gladly burn with these ships that represent the past to which they cannot return.

The activity itself consists of printing out small paper ships and distributing them among participants, several ships for each person. Participants are encouraged to write down, without getting personal, all the things that they would like to burn with the ships as they move on into the 21st century. These can be activities, projects, constraints, frustrations—anything that they would not want to carry with their luggage as they move ahead.

Once this is done (participants should be warned about the nature of the exercise ahead of time), all of the ships will be piled up in the middle in such a way that nobody can tell who wrote what, and then carried either to a symbolic pyre, or, if possible, to a real fire to be read aloud by somebody and then tossed into the fire.

The activity is very powerful, and if it can be done in the evening while gathering around a real fireplace, it can become an incredibly cathartic bonding experience. The reasons are many. All educators always have something to get off their chests, especially in the setting of a school: sometimes it's the bureaucracy of the system, or the excessive shortsighted focus on testing, or any one of a myriad of other evils that the average teacher has to wage a losing battle against every day. And there are seldom any chances to voice these concerns in a safe and anonymous environment. Being able to literally burn their frustrations is not only a welcome chance to blow off steam, but also can help to create a sense of esprit de corps that may very well result in a unified sense of purpose.

The other benefit is that the collection of burned ships can give any administrators and policymakers who are present a rare legitimate glimpse into the feelings of people in the school or district, especially targeting what it is that frustrates them and limits their progress and forward thinking. The safe, anonymous environment offered is a true gateway for legitimate concerns to emerge, and paying close attention, even though there is no hard copy register of what will be burned in the fire, can yield a great set of no-no's for the future.

It is a good idea to engage in this activity sooner rather than later; ideally it could follow the first immersion activity. The burning of the ships conveys the importance of the pivotal moment in education that we are all facing, and it explicitly liberates participants to look forward, emphasizing the need to sever ties with the past.

In this particular activity, it is important that the facilitator does not attempt to round up or summarize what has been said. In general, each reflection carries its own weight. A general final message about how it is a healthy thing that we were able to express ourselves and how there is hope that as we move forward we will really be able to overcome our frustrations can serve as a closing statement.

Role Playing

Another surprisingly powerful catalyst to bringing the vision down into the real world is role playing. Fiction can be a unique prism that allows very serious ideas to surface, since it frees participants from the everyday constraints of implementation, and provides them with a playful environment in which they can shed any inhibitions about what needs to change, since the setting will deliberately place them in a fictional environment in the distant future.

Participants will be challenged to first script and then act out a five-minute rendition of the school of the future. Any scene will do, as long as it reflects something that transpires in school. The time frame for the future can be defined as whenever the foreseeable technology and promises of 21st-century education are materialized. It does not matter when, since the analysis and breakdown of what is acted out will not focus on any specific technique, but rather on the principles; even a very farfetched futuristic situation can yield valuable clues in terms of the underlying collective vision of participants. Presenting a situation far in the future can be a great stress reliever, in that the distance to what is being shown is so great in people's mindsets that they are not at risk of being called out to actually think about implementing their ideas in the near future. The "far into the future" dimension of the activity allows for people to be much more creative and uninhibited in their ideas, which can provide very expressive pointers to the future vision.

It would be useful, if possible, to digitally record all of the scenes acted out and, depending on the number of participants, replay them later in order to analyze what the salient elements of these fictional depictions were.

The subsequent analysis involves breaking the fictional scenarios down into principles that relate to previous reflections on 21st-century education. In general, people open up quite a lot during these role-playing sessions, even the most conservative types. Within the safety of the distant future "blue sky" nature of the activity, people have a greater chance of letting go than in an another more formal setting that may have direct implications.

If the playful mood allows for it, an impromptu awards ceremony can be held, with rewards for best actor, most original script, and so on—perhaps even complete with fake Oscars to be given out.

The ensuing reflection, despite the seemingly lighthearted nature of the activity, can be immensely valuable in the process of discerning the participants' vision for the future. Systematically breaking down the elements that can be observed in these fictional situations can provide a wealth of data as to what people in the group consider to be the main characteristics of the school of the future, which in most cases constitutes a really positive vision that the facilitator can build upon to not only continue the process of consolidating the vision, but also to create a really positive expectation for that future.

Completing the Phrases

Another interesting visioning exercise that also attempts to create a playful environment in which participants can truly express themselves, without the concerns and restraints that normally populate more serious pathways for discussion, is a sort of "chocolate Russian roulette." Participants will work in small groups, and each small group will receive a box of chocolates. Each chocolate will have a piece of paper taped to its bottom, so that participants will pick a chocolate randomly from the box without knowing what is attached to it.

Once people have selected their chocolates, they will have to extract the piece of paper from the underside. Some pieces of paper may be blank, and those participants can just enjoy their chocolates, but most contain a phrase to be completed. If there is a phrase, it must be completed out loud within the group before the participant eats the chocolate.

All of the phrases will nudge participants to express their thoughts about the future. Examples may include:

- My dream for the school/district in the future is . . .

- My concern regarding 21st-century implementation is . . .

- In the future, I would like our school/district to be able to . . .

- As a wild idea, I would suggest that . . .

- Would it be impossible to . . .

- What if we . . .

- My greatest aspiration for the future is that our students . . .

One person in the group can serve as note-keeper and compile a document that consolidates all of these reflections, which the facilitator can share in a plenary session, or simply make available as part of the final document.

Questions

This activity is similar to the "completing the phrases" activity. Each small group will be presented with photographs that depict various situations related to the challenge of 21st-century learning. The photographs are presented face down. Taking turns, each participant will turn over one of the photographs, choose one card that contains a lead-up to a question (how, what, where, when, can, should), and write a question on the back of the photograph. Subsequently, each participant will ask the rest of the group for other questions that pertain to the photograph. Answers are strictly forbidden!

During breaks, workshop coordinators will type up these questions and share a presentation showing each of the photographs with the attached questions.

Compiling the Vision

At the end of a series of visioning activities designed to get participants into a thinking mode and to encourage them to stretch beyond the conditioned responses of typical professional development settings, leaders in the school or district will have compiled a series of invaluable reflections, thoughts, ideas, and other expressions of the collective vision for the future of faculty and other staff in the organization.

These reflections will definitely not yield a strategic plan or even a series of steps, but they can constitute a wonderful first step in bringing the vision down from the sky-high view that is typical of any visioning exercise. If used well, this first compilation can serve as a starting point to developing and deploying a 21st-century curriculum, with the added benefit that it will have stemmed out of the spontaneous views of the practitioners—a rarity in educational practice—which can definitely help legitimize the whole process.

CHAPTER THREE

A Pedagogy for Lifelong Learning

In the context of a totally redefined knowledge paradigm that has completely overturned the rules of the game when it comes to instruction, it follows naturally that it is not only necessary to overhaul and redevelop the curriculum, but, equally importantly, to come up with new methods of delivery that target the new curricular drivers and main principles of 21st-century education.

The traditional pedagogy is mostly geared to addressing the needs and outcomes of the pre-Internet era: in a context in which the teacher was the sole possessor of knowledge and the indispensable link to learning, it made sense that everything was centered around the overpowering figure and influence of the educator in the front of the room. At a time when knowledge was more static, the skill required of the teachers was that they be able to pass along that knowledge within a top-down model, making it engaging and clear enough that students could learn from them. Because students had to learn from the teacher, and were expected to learn the same way the teacher learned, it also followed that assessments were largely focused on a one-size-fits-all model that mirrored the mode of learning. The other revered part of the learning process—the textbook—provided a supplementary source of knowledge, and the related pedagogy unwittingly honored the timeless tradition of memorizing sections of the book to be regurgitated during the written summative end-of-unit test.

Successive courses of study occurred under the same model, and formal education was a continuous sequence of teachers imparting knowledge. The skills students needed for that scenario are all too familiar: summarizing, note-taking, listening. Two kinds of learners were favored above all others: the good listeners—those who could sit for a long time in a room listening to oral explanations and make sense of them; and the proficient readers—the ones who could read and decode long chunks of text, successfully sorting out the important information for later use in evaluations.

The model was carefully honed over the years with a very explicit goal of accumulating knowledge and becoming self-sufficient learners on their way to higher degrees of specialization that would require increased difficulty of the content, a narrower focus, and the need to remember as much as possible, all within a context that relied almost exclusively on individual contributions.

As we have already mentioned, the new knowledge paradigm challenges many of these preconceptions, literally changing most of the axioms in the model. The main objective of formal schooling is to provide students with the skills and, even more importantly, with the internal motivation to become lifelong learners. Even though learning content is still important to provide a foundation for higher-order thinking and to cultivate well-informed and conversant citizens, the focus of a 21st-century curriculum is on the acquisition of skills, many of them completely new skills that befit the new paradigm of a networked, infinite knowledge scenario.

In the face of such a massive change in the main objective of formal schooling, a completely new pedagogy needs to be defined. The vertical, top-down model of the teaching and learning process in the old school is automatically defunct when fostering independent learning is the principal goal. The infinite learning playground that calls for teachers to redefine themselves as learners alongside their own students, acknowledging joyfully that they are no longer absolutely responsible for passing down the learning, requires new methods of delivery, new assessments, and even a new lexicon to describe what goes on in school. Some terms that may be outdated in the new context of ubiquitous, continuous learning are: instruction, the classroom, testing, and the automatic use of the word "teach" in every phrase that relates to learning.

Once again, there is not and there will never be a standard 21st-century pedagogy. In an intrinsically dynamic environment defined by fast-paced changes, even though the principles that focus on independent learning are immutable, the skills and the content needed will be changing all the time, and new tools and techniques will be available for use within the learning environment.

The following sections all address the development of a new, 21st-century pedagogy based on the principles outlined in the previous chapters, with the main focus on capitalizing on the promises of 21st-century education and making lifelong learning the most important objective of school. What follows is by no means a prescribed, universal set of rules guaranteed to deliver a 21st-century curriculum; rather, this chapter offers some possible ways in which we can change traditional delivery methods in order to allow our students to develop the skills and the motivation needed to become independent learners.

The Elephant in the Room: Rigor

Before we try to define at length some of the possible incarnations of a 21st-century pedagogy, it is imperative that we at least address an important underlying issue in the whole discussion. The notion of developing a 21st-century curriculum—designing and implementing innovative practices in education—has seemingly been at odds with the notion of a rigorous curriculum and/or "academic excellence."

The preconception is that curricular practices that take time and effort away from teaching content and achieving exacting fixed outcomes will somehow detract from the general rigor of the academic environment. The point is well taken. It cannot be denied that rote

learning and teaching to the test will yield results that are better targeted to obtaining good standardized test scores, and that many of the
ideas that will be suggested are mostly directed to the learning of skills
that will serve students well in the context of the 21st century, but that,
paradoxically, are generally not measured or assessed in any of the in-
cumbent assessment systems present in most schooling systems all
over the United States and the rest of the world.

Even without entering the realm of standardized testing, rigor
is generally conceived by educators as high-level performance on
academic tasks that, more often than not, are geared toward content
mastery and proficiency at some conventional skills. Some of the characteristics of the "old school" have meticulously evolved through a
sort of natural selection process to ensure that students put in an effort to study more, do their homework, learn their drills, etc. The
heavy emphasis on grades, for example, is an important part of the
carrots-and-sticks environment that rewards students for good performance on the assessment system and punishes those who fail.

The notion of the Gauss curve seems to be deeply rooted in student DNA, in that students implicitly and sometimes explicitly acknowledge that not all students in a class can be successful. When I
tell my students that they will be able to hand in assignments repeatedly until they correct all their mistakes, and that I will only assign
them a grade after they have responded to all corrections, almost invariably somebody raises the issue that is in everybody's minds: that
if they go on improving their assignments until they have perfected
them, then every student would get top marks. Students say this as if
it were almost blasphemous to the essence of assessment itself. Our
own professional preconceptions can attest to this fact: when we know
of a teacher whose students are all getting extremely good grades
within the internal marking system, to our instinctive, judgmental
selves, it reeks of complacency.

It all goes back to redefining the notion of success and, consequently, of a rigorous environment conducive to such success. If our

expected outcome is apprehension of content and facts, and mastery of certain fixed concepts, then a rigorous curriculum is one that delivers on those expectations and, as such, gauges whether students have accumulated the knowledge and acquired the skills that go along with them. However, if success is synonymous with lifelong learning, and, furthermore, with being a self-motivated lifelong learner, then the skills to be held accountable for and the content to be learned will be totally different, and will give shape to a new definition of a rigorous curriculum.

The mindset change needed is related to reassessing the highest-order priorities of the school curriculum, and redefining what is essential in the learning process. If we do more than just paying lip service to the learning of the new skills, then academic excellence will be embodied by curiosity, creativity, resourcefulness, searching for information, and the ability and desire to learn beyond school. It is certainly hard, but we need to get over our obsession with hard, fixed, measurable outcomes as markers for school success. In that context, the elephant in the room vanishes and the tension between rigor and educational innovation can be reconciled.

The Traditional Learning Sequence in the Old Pedagogy

Even though, of course, no two lessons are the same and every teacher does things in a different way, the traditional learning sequence in the "old school" typically followed a certain pattern. One of the basic tenets that provided the foundation for such a pedagogy had to do with the fact that it was thought that content mastery should be acquired before proficiency at tasks was attempted. There was a linearity to the procedure based on the accumulation and concatenation of increasingly complex knowledge, with an assessment that generally happened at the end of each unit.

The traditional sequence would look like this:

1. **Content.** In some form or other, the teacher would introduce the content to students, the most frequent incarnation being the teacher lecturing at the front of the classroom and/or relying on the textbook to assist in the learning. These lessons had, as their main objective, for the teacher to be able to pass on the knowledge to students, placing a high value on how the teacher could be engaging in the explanation, reach out to many students, and use a variety of methods to get the message across. The learning process was clearly asymmetrical and top-down: the teacher taught and the students learned.

2. **Assignments.** As a prelude to the final, more formal, and most important summative assessment, students were exposed to different assignments that were used to consolidate the learning and to offer practice within a less threatening environment than that of the written end-of-unit test. Depending on the subject matter in question, the nature of the assignments was such that students would reinforce their content knowledge and fine-tune their skills while doing them. When there wasn't enough time during class to do them under the guidance and supervision of the teacher, they would form part of the venerable and long-argued-over homework.

3. **End-of-Unit Evaluation.** If the unit stretched too long in time or was excessively long in terms of content, an intermediate evaluation would act as a checkpoint in order to break down what needed to be learned, but otherwise students were assessed via the traditional end-of-unit test. Surely the most common of all assessment species, the legendary final summative assess-

ments shared certain characteristics irrespective of physical location, type of school, and age of the students. They were fixed in time—that is, learning had to occur and students had to be ready for the precise moment in which the evaluation was administered. Learning was strictly individual, so much so that the phrase "we are under test conditions" strikes a chord with anybody who has gone through school. Students gradually became masterful at preparing for these tests, which dominated and impacted the scope and extent of the learning process more than anything else in school. The standard battle cry of any student when confronted with a new topic in a class was "will this be on the test?" and if the teacher dared confess that something would *not* be included on the test, that topic was irreversibly condemned to oblivion. These summative assessments would, of course, be graded, and that particular mark had, in general, a big influence on the student's grade for the marking period in question. Very little or no reflection was indulged in when the tests were returned; students expressed themselves spontaneously as happy or sad depending on the grade awarded, and, at most, analysis of the evaluation, which took place an extended period of time after it was taken, was done for purely utilitarian reasons, such as checking on whether the teacher had added points correctly, or if any inconsistencies in the marking could allow the students to complain in hopes of a better grade.

4. **New Unit.** After the sequence was completed, the teacher would move on to a new unit, in some cases related to or built upon the knowledge of the previous unit, and the sequence would start all over again, with

very little or no reflection on the learning process and whether the first unit's learning goals had been accomplished or not.

It is clear that the "old school" process as described is an unfair generalization of teachers' efforts, and that many of these somewhat retrograde practices have resulted as a consequence of large class sizes, reduced paid time for preparation and marking assessments, and difficult working conditions for teachers in general. However, most of the salient elements of this old sequence are still fairly common in today's classrooms. Even acknowledging that some of those characteristics are rather exaggerated in the preceding description, even attenuated versions of such pedagogical approaches are totally counter to the 21st-century challenge and are not compatible with the development and deployment of a 21st-century curriculum.

The New Sequence: Learning on Time vs. Lifelong Learning

The new learning environment—a renewed knowledge paradigm of infinitely available information and the recognition that lifelong learning is the primary goal of the educational system—creates the need for a new method of delivery, one that is more consistent with the changed goals of the educational system and formal schooling, as well as with the current context for educators and the challenges they face.

If we were to compare and contrast the old pedagogy with the new pedagogy, we would immediately find the old pedagogy not only lacking in its ability to provide students with the right settings and incentives to learn, but also quite contradictory to some of the basic tenets of the new educational model. By analyzing some of the shortcomings of the previous model, we can gain some very valuable insights into some of the principles upon which we should base a new pedagogy.

To start with, it should almost be self-evident by this time that the classroom-based, traditional, teacher-centered scenario is not conducive to fostering lifelong learning and instilling habits of independent learning. That does not mean that the teacher should be totally absent from the learning process, or that students should learn entirely on their own, but rather that the role of the teacher should be converted into a far more valuable one than that of just regurgitating secondhand knowledge.

Another fundamental flaw of the old pedagogy has to do with the fixed-in-time nature of assessments. The tradition of testing all students at the same time and to the same expectations followed some logically desired outcomes of education in the postindustrial world, when instruction was extended to the masses, and teachers had to deal with increasing class sizes. But we now understand that although it makes assessments more difficult to implement in real life, evaluation should not be one-size-fits-all in its approach and uniform in terms of expectations. In the merciless environment that allowed no retests, students had one chance only to demonstrate their proficiency and knowledge, taking place at a precise moment in time. A more flexible assessment scheme that allows for multiple opportunities for success and that is not so fixated on time would permit students who learn at different paces to be successful.

The lack of reflection opportunities in which students explicitly try to assess their own learning, understand where they erred, and receive timely and relevant feedback about how to improve their learning is also a major shortcoming of the old model that needs to form the core of the new pedagogy.

Surprisingly, one of the major assumptions about knowledge acquisition, namely that we need to learn stuff before we are able to do stuff, has been called into question. Authors Bernie Trilling and Charles Fadel account for this paradoxical change in their book *21st Century Skills: Learning for Life in Our Times* (2009): "Recent research in cognition, the science of thinking, has punctured a time-honored tenet of teaching: that mastering contents must precede putting them to good use."

Freeing teachers from the need to engage in noncontextual explanations in order to break down the theoretical background leading to practical applications suddenly provides them with a very powerful tool to make their lessons more appealing. With the logical exception of dangerous procedures (you would not want your child to take an inquiry-based approach to mixing sodium with water in a chemistry lesson), educators can now have their students learn by doing, using project- and problem-based learning activities that are more relevant to their lives—and a lot more fun.

A pedagogy that addresses learning as the major goal and not just complying with fixed curriculum requirements needs perforce to break away from some of the standard practices that have been omnipresent in classrooms for ages. Some of the suggested building blocks for a new pedagogy presented in the next section are general principles and trends, not specific recommendations. Each suggestion can be tailored to the age and cognitive ability of students and can be adapted to different disciplines. They are presented as a series of elements that build upon some of the basic axioms of 21st-century education, so even in this dynamic era they should serve students well by preparing them to meet some of the yet-unknown expectations of this no-longer nascent century.

The Salient Elements of a 21st-Century Pedagogy

Freely Available Content

Despite the die-hard determination and multimillion-dollar efforts of content providers, one of the quintessential characteristics of the post-Internet world is that all content is available and that attempts to artificially contain the widespread dissemination of information are absolutely futile and a waste of time.

The fact that nearly all accumulated human knowledge is just a few keystrokes away presents a formidable challenge in itself, in that students must filter overwhelming amounts of information in order to find and distinguish what is relevant. This fact also means that the protected environment in which students were spoon-fed carefully selected content that had been vetted by the teacher needs to gradually give way to progressively exposing students to the open content that is freely available on the Internet.

This poses the challenge of helping students learn how to sort through the maze and find what is scientifically accurate and from a reliable source. Being able to do that is an important real-life skill; when students engage in lifelong learning that is not anchored in any formal schooling, they will be on their own and the trend toward increasing available content will likely not slow down, but propagate at an even higher rate.

Accomplishing this involves utilizing, as classroom materials and references for the learning process, as many resources as possible that are freely available online, and doing so with increasing frequency as students get older and acquire greater mastery at filtering.

Progressively more intense exercises based on tapping into the limitless information on the Internet can also help students reconcile the new notion of knowledge. In the past, when access to publishing was not almost cost free as it is today, allowing any blogger to proclaim themselves an expert on any topic, we were shielded against incorrect, biased, or ill-intentioned information by virtue of the barriers to publishing, peer reviews, and other processes that scrutinized texts before they saw the light of day.

In the current free-for-all environment in which anybody can reach a massive global audience, the concept of knowledge has changed. The authors of the original encyclopedias in France back in the 1700s sought to summarize in a few volumes all of the knowledge of the era. Now such a feat would be unthinkable.

David Weinberger (2012) specifically addresses the issue of how knowledge can be defined in the Internet era:

We are inescapably facing the fact that the world is too big to know. And as a species we are adapting. Our traditional knowledge-based institutions are taking their first hesitant steps on land, and knowledge is beginning to show its new shape: This is not a mere thought experiment. It is what the Internet is doing to knowledge. The Internet simply doesn't have what it takes to create a body of knowledge: No editors and curators who get to decide what is in or out. No agreed-upon walls to let us know that knowledge begins here, while outside uncertainty reigns—at least none that everyone accepts.

Exposing students as much as possible to the world of content available online will help them gain invaluable discernment skills for the future and, even more importantly, to confront the inherent uncertainty of the new knowledge paradigm with confidence and without fear.

Classroom Without Walls

Advances in telecommunications and in the myriad of electronic tools at our disposal, which are continually becoming more powerful and ubiquitous, have effectively torn down the four walls of the classroom. That metaphor has been used a great deal, and it is quite apt. If we were physically standing in a room with no walls, we would be hard pressed to always remain within the confines of the room.

There are countless resources on the Internet containing lectures, live interactivity, and a score of other possible gateways that can take students beyond our own limited knowledge and expertise, and students would benefit from globalized access to these resources. It is almost inconceivable that students are not exposed more regularly to some of the interactions and external resources freely available on the Internet. The world at large does not hesitate to expose students to the material that pundits and bloggers think is important: celebrity gossip, video game reviews, political rants, viral videos; so schools certainly should not hesitate to expose students to resources that educators think are important.

It would not be unreasonable to expect, at this point in time, that tapping into the wealth of knowledge and the wonderful resources that await on the Internet should be an essential element in any classroom at any age level. Having, literally, an outside voice in the classroom not only would alleviate some of the pressure on the teacher but also would present students with a greater variety of teaching styles, and students would benefit from professionally generated learning materials and world-class speakers.

"Open Book" Assessments

Another artificial constraint within the traditional education system is that assessments are "closed book." There are a few professions that require real-time high levels of performance, such as fighter pilots, astronauts, and surgeons, but otherwise it is extremely rare for a person to have to perform without being able to access the Internet or another source to assist them with the task at hand.

Open-book assessments should be the norm rather than the exception, if we want to prepare students for the world they will be living in. Open book, in the online era, means open Internet, and it is up to the teacher to create assessments that target the learning of higher-order skills so that the Internet can be a medium to supplement those skills in an environment that mirrors the real-life scenario of continuous learning. This implies, of course, that we must take a long, hard look at our assessment instruments, which probably need to be refocused so as to target the learning of, and later demonstration of proficiency on, tasks that are very different from the traditional model.

Collaborative Learning

One of the most flagrant disconnects between the old model of education and the current reality is that most activities in school, and most assessments, are targeted toward individual work and individual accountability. In almost every occupation, collaborative work is the standard mode of operation, and people have to learn the hard way how to be functional, active, and valuable members of the team when they have left the formal school environment.

A prominent feature of the 21st-century classroom is that students must learn to work collaboratively and also must be assessed in terms of their individual contributions to the group, as well as in terms of the performance of the group as a whole. Rubrics should address not just how each team member can contribute in a unique way to the best of their potential, but also how the group has fared as a consequence of those individual contributions. From a very early age, students should be regularly acquiring the skills to function as an effective team member, one of the most desired and most frequently advertised traits in job descriptions.

Teachers are always on the lookout for students who hide behind the group to mask their lack of effort, and are quick to break up markedly asymmetrical, mixed-ability teams, so that the "lazy" students can't piggyback on the work done by the better students in the group. However, tasks should be assigned in such a way that students with different abilities and learning styles can significantly contribute to the production of the group in ways that are relevant and that can be reflected in the final product and ensuing assessment.

Thomas and Seely Brown (2011) make explicit reference to this vastly unappreciated and underutilized resource:

> Take, for instance, one of the most difficult and dreaded classroom activities: the group project. Students struggle to complete the exercise and teachers struggle to grade it. Why? Because our models of how a classroom works have no way

of understanding, measuring, or evaluating collectives. Even worse, they have no means of understanding how notions of the personal may engage students. As a result, group work is almost always evaluated by assigning individual grades to students based on their contribution. What goes unrecognized is the fact that when groups work well, the result is usually a product of more than the sum of individual achievements. Even if a teacher does acknowledge that phenomenon and assign one grade to the entire group, the impulse is still to reward individual achievement (or in some cases punish the lack of it).

Even as obvious and as blatant as this is, there is, as of yet, no vocal push by educators to convert the prevailing pedagogy to one where collaborative learning is what happens most often within the learning process. It should be noted, however, that collaboration is one of the real-life building blocks of the new knowledge paradigm, and, as such, should also form part of the foundation of any school curriculum in the 21st century and should be a defining element of the new pedagogy.

Continuous Formative Assessment

The traditional "old school" education model mostly relies on end-of-unit summative assessments to gauge student performance. Despite extensive efforts to try to reshape assessment practices in school systems all over the world, this final do-or-die formal evaluation still remains largely the dominant assessment type. The problems associated with end-of-unit assessments are very obvious and easy to relate to a real-life experience in the classroom. When handed back these evaluations, students seldom take more than a cursory look at them to see what grade they received. There is no actual feedback on the learning process; mistakes are viewed as detrimental to the grade but not as information that can improve understanding and mastery.

Within a 21st-century learning environment, it is imperative that formative assessment become the norm. The positive impact of formative assessments on student learning is well known; formative assessment allows students to receive timely feedback that enables them to learn from their mistakes in ways that are nonthreatening and that allow them opportunities to improve their work.

In particular, technology and the electronic medium lend themselves very well to this type of assessment. E-mail, or blogs where students post their assignments, allow the teacher to view student work multiple times and give them feedback, so that students can continuously improve their work until they have done it satisfactorily. This is not only efficient from an environmental point of view, since a lot of paper will be saved in the process, but also addresses one of the most important principles upon which a successful educational program should be built: that students feel that they are successful.

We need to remember that the education model that favors end-of-unit summative assessments was born from the necessity of remembering content and from a curriculum that was heavily built upon factual recall. The fact that there is no longer a dire need to remember so much content allows for different forms of assessment that can be less lengthy and formal, and more ubiquitous and continuous.

Self-Assessment as a Key Skill Needed for Lifelong Learning

Self-assessment has been present in classrooms forever, and it has sometimes been ridiculed as an effort on the part of the teacher to unload some of their tasks on students, as if these well-intentioned attempts to teach students the skill of assessing their own learning were only intended to save the teacher correction time.

In the context of lifelong learning, self-assessment has an all-important status. When learning on our own, without the presence of a teacher, mentor, or facilitator, being able to self-assess how much we know, whether we have mastered contents and skills, what we are lacking, and, eventually, how to go about learning the things we are lacking, are essential building blocks in the independent learning process.

Because of this, self-assessment needs to be learned from an early age, and progressively infused within curricular practices at school. This is nothing new to teachers, who have dabbled at teaching students this form of assessment for ages. But now, within the 21st-century learning scenario, educators need to understand that this is no longer just an occasional exercise but rather an essential skill that students have to acquire.

Using the Internet and Technology for Learning

One of the biggest hurdles that has to be overcome in the heretofore not very successful marriage between technology and schools is that the implementation of technology within schools has mostly been geared toward enhancing teaching. Many of the hardware options that are available for schools (interactive whiteboards, overhead projectors, document cameras, PowerPoint presentations) glorify and perpetuate the teacher-centered model of education.

Education can only be truly revolutionized by technology through the use of software and hardware for learning. The real breakthrough comes when we empower the learning process through this most powerful of catalysts. When students who have been long exposed to the traditional model of education are asked to use the Internet for learning, surprisingly, they find it incredibly hard. It seems that there is some sort of profound internal dissociation of the use of the Internet for learning. Teenagers associate the Internet with socializing and fun, and other than conventional searches on Google for research purposes, they do not have the tools or the ingrained reflexes to be able to learn from videos, simulations, tutorials, or other interactive Internet sources.

In a true 21st-century pedagogy, it is extremely important that students be exposed progressively to more intensive use of the Internet for learning. Students need to be able to tap into the nearly infinite resources online almost intuitively.

Another trait students need to develop is an innate curiosity that makes them seek to learn continuously, and that makes good on the new realization that learning is really ubiquitous. When I started teaching, mentors told me that the worst thing that a teacher could do is to try to "fake it" in a situation in which a student asked a question that the teacher didn't know the answer to. I was told that the right answer in that situation was "I don't know." These days, there is no excuse to stop at "I don't know." Now it is important that we model the "learn right now" attitude. The answer we should give now is "I don't know . . . let's Google it and find out."

Modeling the immediacy of learning is not enough, however. One fundamental trait of a lifelong learner is the thirst for knowledge—the desire to learn. I often do an experiment with my students. I show them a short video of a technological innovation that amazes them; for example, the TED video that explains how a group of researchers at MIT have developed a wearable device called SixthSense that is able to provide real-time information on anything, from humans to household goods in the supermarket (Mistry, 2009). After the video concludes, I tell them that, in an unprecedented event, I will be giving them 10 minutes to do whatever they please, on two conditions: they cannot talk to each other, and at the end of the 10 minutes they must truthfully share with the rest of the class what they have chosen to do during the free time. The objective of the exercise, of course, is to see how many of them actually go on the Internet to search for information about this innovation that has just left them with their mouths open, to see if it was further developed, if it is available currently, if progress has been made, and so on. My experience with teenagers is that most of them make use of this precious opportunity to play games or do other stuff that is usually not allowed at school, and only a small percentage of them use any of the time to satisfy their curiosity about the video that they have just watched.

What I seek to impress upon them is that being proficient with the tools and having access to the Internet is not enough: that they need to develop an instinctive, insatiable desire to learn; that they need to take advantage of the immediacy and prevalence of learning; that they need to leave no stone unturned in their quest for knowledge; that they need to access knowledge straightaway, as a spontaneous and natural process.

In order to change the preconception that the Internet is somewhat disassociated from formal learning, the use of the Internet as a source and a learning tool should be progressively encouraged so that students not only acquire the skills to make good use of it, but also end up finding themselves instantly drawn to the online resources as their first stop for learning anything.

Metacognition and Analysis

A relatively new feature of the 21st-century classroom is the need to include time for reflection, analysis of the learning process, and metacognition. With the focus on lifelong learning as the most important goal in education, learners must develop an awareness of the extent and the deficiencies of their learning.

Within the traditional pedagogy, in which the evaluation of learning was heavily teacher-centered and external to the learner, students could be passive subjects in the experience and could expect to be guided, rewarded, and walked through the learning process by adults.

If we want to prepare students to continue learning beyond formal schooling, it is paramount that they develop an acute awareness of where they stand within the learning process. In this context, the 21st-century pedagogy must include specific, intentional activities for each unit of study that facilitate the learners' reflection process. These may include:

• A collective or individual reflection on how much students know about a topic before it's studied. Doing this can help the teacher gauge how much students know about a particular topic, but the main point of the activity is developing the ingrained reflex of assessing one's own knowledge about a topic prior to engaging in the learning. Before setting out to know more about a particular topic, it should be a natural habit for students to assess themselves to determine what they already know, in order to be able to frame the subsequent learning and adapt it to their needs.

• A reflection to help students understand the extent and the depth of the learning process required to gain the proficiency or the level of mastery being sought. This would help measure the breadth of the gap between what students know and what they are expected to know, as well as paving the way for the ensuing learning activities.

• Asking questions. Having students formulate questions related to what they perceive they don't know about the topic also constitutes a good exercise in terms of increasing their awareness of what they need to learn, and of whether they are able to ask educated questions or not.

• An end-of-unit reflection on the learning process. Once the unit is completed, it may also prove valuable to engage students in a discussion about whether the learning objectives were met, to what extent they have mastered the topic, and what else they would need to learn.

In general, reflection should be far more prevalent in the learning process so that students develop the skills, the habits, and the reflexes to be good judges of their own learning, and so that they come to appreciate from an early age that learning is not an automatic process, that they are not merely passive receptors in the teaching and learning equation, and that they all, collectively and individually, have a measure of control of their own learning.

Learning of New Skills

In a 21st-century pedagogy, planning the learning experience for the students should explicitly target the acquisition of 21st-century skills as an inextricable part of every subject. Since we acknowledge that there are certain core 21st-century skills that are essential, based on the fundamental principles of the new knowledge paradigm, we must plan a method of instruction that incorporates lessons in which the students are actively exercising the skills.

The implications are clear. Information should not be delivered in a top-down, spoon-fed fashion, but rather actively garnered by the students themselves, processed, and presented in ways that are relevant to the context in which students will live and continue learning.

Games in the Classroom

In a pedagogy that targets student engagement, the use of games in the classroom, until now only marginally successful in its implementation, should have an increased and more important role.

Later sections of this book focus on how games can become one of the most effective embodiments of a 21st-century curriculum. Gaming and simulations should undoubtedly become one of the most salient and visible elements of the new pedagogy.

Neuroscience Applications

Perhaps the one feature of the 21st-century pedagogy that offers the most promise to truly revolutionize the way we learn is related to practical applications of neuroscience research that help teachers understand how different students learn and how to customize the instructional process so as to take advantage of each child's potential.

Neuroscience is still in its infancy. Though there have been major breakthroughs in the understanding of the inner workings of the brain, there are still few concrete applications that can be used by teachers to significantly enhance the learning process. However, some of the findings in this field are gradually finding their way into software that helps diagnose learning difficulties and adjust the curriculum accordingly. Neuroscience is slowly making its way toward impacting every student.

The potential of neuroscience-based pedagogical improvements is unlimited, and we can expect that in the future there will be a customized curriculum for different learning profiles, and that brain-based strategies will form part of the everyday educational landscape.

Use, Decoding, and Production of Multimedia

To prepare our students for the real world, a 21st-century pedagogy, without disregarding writing, must frequently include multimedia as a preferred medium for learning and also to showcase the results of that learning via student assignments.

There are undoubted benefits to the traditional focus on reading and writing, and, if anything, the overabundance of information results in this being a time when much more needs to be read than ever before. But whether we like it or not, our students are going to be increasingly exposed to multimedia, and will be required to express themselves in their future workplaces via multimedia presentations or even the production of videos.

If the school environment wants to mirror real life, then, a 21st-century pedagogy must include multimedia as a form of delivering the learning, as well as demonstrating the learning. This involves finding resources such as videos, interactive tutorials, and multimedia presentations that can serve as the basis for the learning process, and having students present their work not only in writing but also through multimedia. And it cannot be stressed enough that the way students express themselves through multimedia should also form part of the assessment process. Teachers should react to a poorly designed multimedia presentation with the same horror that they express when confronted with very bad grammar or blatant spelling mistakes.

Formal and Informal Learning

Probably one of the most controversial and difficult aspects of creating a 21st-century pedagogy has to do with acknowledging that learning does not only occur within the formal learning environment. Educators have long known but rarely acknowledged that there are very significant learning experiences to be gained outside of the classroom, within many of the extracurricular activities, sports, and other programs that complement the academic experience at the school.

Living proof of this is that when students are asked as they leave school, or even many years later, what some of their most memorable experiences were, they very often point to things that have transpired outside of the classroom. And, even though it may be argued that an event having a place in the fond recollections of the students does not necessarily mean that significant learning took place, there is also an element of wisdom in the idea that even very young students can intuitively discern quite clearly what has had a large and positive impact on their lives.

There is abundant research on how sports, drama, and other nonacademic activities shape character, build values, and teach very valuable lessons that transcend the learning of content and skills in the academic arena. If we add to this the fact that learning can take place anywhere and everywhere, and that disciplines are being reassessed in terms of their value in the context of the 21st century, a distinctive feature of a 21st-century school is that informal learning is recognized explicitly in terms of its very important contribution to the overall education of students at the school.

In his seminal book *Informal Learning: Rediscovering the Natural Pathways That Inspire Innovation and Performance* (2006), author Jay Cross explicitly addresses the issue of how a learning strategy must incorporate explicitly the informal learning process: "We've outgrown the definition of learning as the activity of an individual and moved back to an apprenticeship model, though at a higher level. We learn in context, with others, as we live and work. Recognizing this fact is the first step to crafting an effective learning strategy."

The change in mindset required has to do with accepting that informal learning occurs, that it is a valuable part of the school curriculum, and that, even if there are difficulties regarding how to measure the effectiveness of that learning, and how much students actually learn, parts of school life that catalyze informal learning should be intentionally included and regarded as an important part of the curriculum.

The New Sequence

After going through some of the characteristics of a 21st-century pedagogy, a new related challenge emerges as a consequence of the realization that embedded in some of those visible manifestations of a new method of delivery, there are new fundamental building blocks for the teaching and learning process: the development of a new pedagogical sequence that supersedes the old traditional one.

In the traditional learning sequence, the overarching objective of the process was for students to acquire knowledge, and, almost as an afterthought or byproduct, for them to develop certain skills. In the 21st-century context, the importance of those objectives is reversed. Content, activities, and assessments should serve as media through which students can acquire skills, habits, and deeper motivation geared to lifelong learning.

A precise sequence or series of steps cannot be postulated in the context of a dynamically changing world, and there is no single right answer when it comes to determining what is the best way to infuse 21st-century practices into curriculum with the goal of having the students learn new skills. The suggested sequence that follows is just one possibility; it is a very general set of ideas as to how best to foster the development of 21st-century skills.

The first consideration is that the new "sequence" is not a linear sequence, in which each step happens in order and a logical outcome follows. As is evident in Figure 3.1, a pedagogical strategy that addresses the issue of 21st-century learning is more cyclical in its nature.

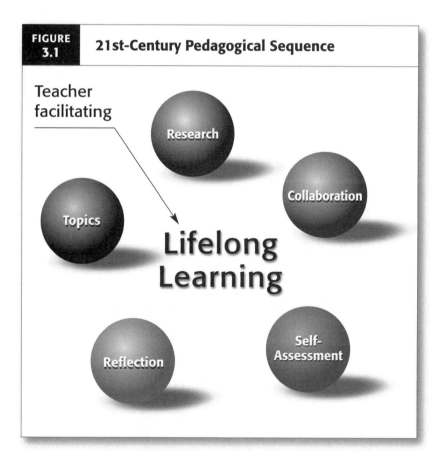

FIGURE 3.1   21st-Century Pedagogical Sequence

Topics. Introducing the topics is still a logical first stage in terms of getting students ready for the learning that will take place. However, contrary to the old model in which the teacher would carefully explain the intricacies of the topics and skills included in the unit, in the new model topics should be presented as a general introduction in order to jump-start an initial discussion or reflection on what will be studied. It is always a good idea to explore the previous knowledge of the students, both as a way to tap into that knowledge itself, modeling the fact that learning is not a top-down activity but rather a collaborative one, and as a natural first step toward reflecting about how much we know, and what else needs to be known.

Even though reflection is included as one stage in the process, it should be clearly stated that reflection must be omnipresent throughout the whole process, since reflecting on one's own learning is an integral and essential part of the lifelong learning process.

Research. The bread and butter of lifelong learning is actively researching what needs to be learned, preferably online and with unrestricted content so that students can learn how to use the Internet in a systematic and educated way that not only is efficient in its approach and the utilization of the tools available, but also targeted specifically toward the learning that needs to take place. In this respect, the research stage should be scientifically learned, so that students can gradually take a very general idea on the topic, narrow it down to the most important information, and converge upon the desired learning outcomes. Whenever possible this stage should be self-directed, and students should be able to evaluate whether they have enough knowledge or information based on their initial reflections about determining the learning goals.

Collaboration. Also present during the whole process, collaboration should be the norm in a 21st-century pedagogy. Students need to learn the skills associated with collaboration in order to become functional in the everyday world. Also, collaborative research will help students specialize in one particular area, or else utilize their combined research to "predigest" the vast amounts of information available for better use by the group. Assessments should not just target individual students, but also should include, within the rubric, a component that accounts for the collective group effort in a way that emphasizes the importance of contributing to the team, even if for the purely selfish reason of wanting to get a higher grade.

Self-Assessment. A formal and well-documented self-assessment process needs to take place so that students can make real-time decisions about their own learning and are empowered to go back to the cycle and retrace some of their previous steps in order to achieve the learning objectives. Self-assessment is not limited to the individual; it should also be part of the team learning experience. An interesting exercise consists of having student groups develop a rubric that gauges the degree to which the team has been able to master the topic and/or complete the assignment, analyze the conclusions, and then go back to the learning process to improve the outcomes.

Reflection. Throughout the learning process students should be encouraged to reflect on whether they have accomplished the learning objectives, what they still need to learn, and the limitations of what they have learned so far, with the ultimate goal of generating in our students reflexes and habits that help them evaluate their own learning.

The Role of the Teacher

In a 21st-century pedagogy, the role of teachers changes fundamentally from the traditional role, in which they deliver content and are basically in front of the class for most of the learning experience, to a new role, in which they perform tasks conducive to fostering lifelong learning, such as mentoring, helping to research, clarifying questions and doubts, explaining certain difficult content that students may require assistance with, and guiding students through the reflection process.

Asking teachers to step away from the front of the class is not a small change. It requires a fundamental change in disposition in terms of what is perceived to be good teaching, and what is important in terms of teacher expectations. I have taught in a self-induced 21st-century learning environment for several years already, and, when I am most successful, I walk into a class and students practically don't need me. The degree to which I am superfluous is a good indicator of how well the class is going and how well I have accomplished my objectives.

However, the first few times that I did this, I felt ill at ease when I walked into my lesson and had very little to do in the independent learning experience that students were going through. Even though I had instigated the change and was certain that I was ultimately doing my students a good turn by gradually training them to become independent learners, I felt as if I were failing in my profession, and as if I did not add value to the classroom. But soon I found that in the free time that I suddenly had on my hands, I could work with students in small groups or individually to discuss their assignments, and have longer conversations than I previously could have had regarding their progress in school and how well they were doing in my subject. I could address which skills or content I felt needed reinforcement, and even give students guidance in redoing some assignments when it was clear that they were not going to be able to meet the expectations without additional help. What I was doing was what authors have long been advocating in terms of 21st-century education: I was offering a customized curriculum and personalized, timely, and relevant feedback.

Experiencing the changed role of the 21st-century teacher made me realize the extent of the leap of faith that is required for teachers to embrace the new model, and how counterintuitive it can be to move away from the traditional learning sequence. One of the major mistakes we make when advocating for teachers to change their role is that, most often, we stress what they should *not* do: that is, be at the front of the class, explain, and lecture for an extended period of time. However, we seldom focus on what the teacher *can* do when they are not lecturing, and on how that freedom can be put to good use in order to make good on some of the elusive promises of 21st-century education.

CHAPTER FOUR

21st-Century Drivers

The development of the 21st-century school, as would be expected given the magnitude and extent of the transformation required, requires that completely new techniques, tools, and strategies be created and implemented. But, even more importantly, the 21st-century challenge also calls for a new mindset: an open-minded approach to rethinking education in terms of the content and skills to be included within the curriculum, the opportunities for formal and informal learning, the definition of learning, and the necessity of helping students develop the character traits, values, and virtues they need to become fully functional citizens in this new world.

We need creative solutions to provide our students with a well-rounded education. In the pre-Internet era, students' emotional and intellectual learning was made more multidimensional through participation in extracurricular programs that were considered good conduits for the acquisition of the skills, values, and virtues students needed to be good citizens. Popular activities like sports, drama, music, and a multiplicity of after-school clubs provided ample opportunities for students and were powerful catalysts that helped students rise up to their full potential.

The current predicament for education, however, is far more complex, in that it incorporates an undeniable new challenge: how to become proficient users of the powerful technological tools at our disposal in order to gain the profound and long-lasting benefits of productivity, efficiency, and lifelong learning that they make possible while at the same time remaining aware of the ethical implications of the use of such technology, and its inherent risks.

Though it may seem unfair, the responsibility of educating our students in the use of technologies that we ourselves have not planned, developed, or created falls on the shoulders of teachers and the formal school system. Technological devices will continue to be rolled out—each time with increased speed, more processing power, and even more amazing degrees of portability—without regard to their impact on education. The design and production companies' motivation is sales, so it cannot be expected that they will develop an educational program that assists users in becoming responsible and ethical consumers of their products. Whatever new opportunities are opened up as a consequence of the new technologies, it will be left to us, as educators, to pick up the pieces and try to make sense of them.

Matters are further complicated by the fact that young people now in schools lead increasingly more complicated online lives, lives that sometimes become dissociated from their real personas in ways that are unpredictable and difficult to understand for us digital immigrants. Cyber bullying, flaming, and other new manifestations of the traditional social problems that are intrinsically associated with growing up have a strange virtual dimension, and there are countless cases that everyone who has been in the classroom can recall of students who exhibit a totally different behavior online than in real life. Dealing with these issues is not only difficult but also quite counterintuitive for teachers, who generally do not have such an intense and rich online life as their students and consequently cannot relate easily to those experiences.

Contrary to our well-honed reflexes relating to most of the stuff that we teach about, developing the skills and the awareness needed to be intelligent and efficient users of technology cannot be approached simply by coming up with a list of the content and skills to be acquired and interspersing those within the curriculum design. In order to effectively meet this challenge, educators need to first understand the implications of the evolution of technology, its impact on the educational model, and the opportunities and risks it poses. Technology is a very dynamic driver that challenges educators and policymakers to rethink the approach to learning the curriculum and the view of technology as a mere tool. For the younger generation, technology is no longer "technology" but rather just "is"; it is a natural and quintessential part of everyday life that is as ubiquitous as breathing and speaking.

Technology for the Future

Any attempt to predict the future of technology is doomed to fail, given the fast pace of changes and the breathtaking new innovations that are introduced and marketed seemingly every other day. However, in order to rethink the current model of schooling and provide education that allows our students to function effectively in the 21st century, even if the actual devices that will be created cannot be foreseen, it is important to try to anticipate the evolving technological trends and what their long-lasting impact will be on individuals and society.

Of particular interest to schools, of course, is how these new technologies and their evolution will further change the rules of the education game; namely, our real-time searchable access to nearly infinite information.

There are two main areas of technological evolution in the next 20 or 30 years that are bound to alter significantly not only our school systems and the educational paradigm, but also life itself.

The Internet as an Extension of Our Brains

One of these areas of impact is mobile and seamless access to information. There is an irreversible trend for devices to become smaller,

cheaper, and more powerful. Without getting into science fiction scenarios of implanted chips that extend human capabilities, what is now
an incipient trend of continuous access to the Internet will become
even more widespread, bridging the digital divide to extend to more
people regardless of their social and economic standing; it is likely
that in the future, all people will be connected always and everywhere.

If we couple the trends toward faster telecommunication, ease of
access, and reduced costs with the continuous emergence of faster
processors and improved displays with more powerful graphic capability, it seems like we are getting closer to a state where the Internet
will be a natural extension of our brains. This not only will increase
our memory capacity, access to information, and processing power,
but also will mean that we will become not just individuals, but functional parts of the global network at all times.

Rapid advances in the development of wearable devices will likely
lead to an even more seamless integration of technology into our
everyday lives. There are several examples of prototypes currently
being created that will probably hit the market within the next few
years, at accessible costs.

The functions that these devices will perform are a good indication of how technology will evolve in terms of seamless interconnec-
tion. Basically these wearable devices consist of a camera, a computer
microprocessor embedded within the structure of the device, and a
screen that users can read unobstructed as they go about their lives.

One such product is the much hyped "Google Glass," which will
probably see commercial deployment sometime in 2014. These glasses
contain everything the modern smart phone has: a GPS, motion sensors, and high-speed access to the Internet, together with a camera
that can scan the immediate environment to provide for augmented
reality, as well as a small miniature screen that wearers can see from
the corner of their eyes. The device will allow users to interact with
the surrounding environment and will provide real-time information
about it.

The wearable device developed at MIT, SixthSense, has similar capabilities (Mistry, 2009). Just to give an example of how SixthSense works, the user would go to the supermarket, look at a product, which will be scanned and recognized by the camera, and receive almost instantaneous feedback on whatever it is that the user wants to know about that product, whether it be comments by other users, quality, specifications, etc. Even more tantalizing, however, are possibilities regarding the application of augmented reality to the world that surrounds us, including our fellow humans. The concept of augmented reality is already quite current with smart phones, which can direct their cameras to objects or buildings, recognize them, and send back related information. But the real breakthrough will be when we can wear a device that gives us information about other people whom we may not have met before. In a fraction of a second, the device will snap a photograph of the other person, recognize the face, and find his or her name and as much available information as there is on the Internet through Facebook and other media. So even before shaking hands, the owner of the device would know quite a lot of information about the other person.

We are already legitimately concerned about the loss of privacy inherent in having our lives laid out on the Internet, but when these wearable devices become commonplace the threats to our individuality and privacy will be mind-boggling. We would be walking around out in the world with our past records written all over us.

I have had discussions about the powerful and unintended effects of these devices with many groups of high school students. Their reaction is nearly always the same. They are fascinated by the technology, the device, and its potential applications, and yet, despite their youth and near immunity to the fear some adults have toward technological innovations, they are also somewhat horrified at the idea that what now requires a non-real-time effort to go to the Internet to learn as much as possible about a person would become instantaneous and seamless. Students understand the potentially very negative implications of the massive use of such devices. However, when I ask them the defining question about whether they would buy such a device they answer in ways that are emblematic of the problem we educators face when it comes to new technologies. The real question is not whether students, as potential future users of the device, find it threatening and are concerned by the implications. When I ask students if they would buy the device if it were to cost less than $50 and be immediately available in stores, all hands truthfully shoot up, and students say that they would give it a try.

This dilemma is central to all technological developments. When the costs are lowered significantly, the pull of the novelty and even the fact that it may become fashionable to own the device override any rational decisions or concerns over the potential negative uses of such devices, so consumers buy them nonetheless.

The impact on school curriculum of the scenario described presents an almost unfathomable challenge: a curriculum delivered to super-connected users with extended capabilities, which will increasingly become seamlessly available. The implications are quite profound, and will require a new mindset that targets not rote learning but higher-order skills that enable students to tap into the nearly infinite resources available to perform at levels hitherto unreachable by school students.

One key aspect of being able to effectively utilize technology is to be conversant with the underlying principles that constitute the foundations of such tools. Not every person should be able to inspect or correct a search engine algorithm, but a basic understanding of the underlying conceptual mechanism that gives users so much power will be essential so that learners can understand not only the implications and powerful potential uses of such technologies, but also their limitations.

In particular, a thorough knowledge of the inner workings of Web search engines is fundamental to any school curriculum. Students should be able to understand in depth the mechanisms that drive search engines, how information is indexed and catalogued, and how a search engine query is processed and returned.

Even though search engines have opened up a world of unlimited information and are possibly the greatest technological accomplishment of all time, they can also be fooled and manipulated to the advantage of whoever wants their sites to appear at the top of the results list when certain queries are entered. In fact, there are companies that make a very handsome living doing "search engine optimization (SEO)," a carefully thought out set of techniques that target scoring high on certain search engines by modifying the contents of Web sites to that effect.

A standard Google search for SEO will reveal some details about this fascinating service, as well as some other lighter examples of search engine manipulation. Searching in Google for "find Chuck Norris" famously returns at the top of the list a Web site that reads "Google won't search for Chuck Norris because it knows you don't find Chuck Norris, he finds you." Some other Google bombing examples are not so hilarious, such as "Arabian Gulf," "I can read Wikipedia," and "miserable failure," whose returns I will not spoil for inquisitive readers.

It is just common sense to intentionally include the learning of the inner workings of search engines in the curriculum, since students will be using them all their lives and they are likely to become almost second nature to human beings—a natural extension of our brains, memory, and even thought processes.

Artificial Intelligence

The other area that promises to have a significant impact on our everyday lives is the advancement of artificial intelligence. What in the past were laughable attempts to create cumbersome humanoids that were more the stuff of science fiction movies than reality have gradually and almost furtively come of age. Developers have made significant leaps in advancing the processing power of robots and their ability to relate to and interface with human beings in ways that are both fascinating and somewhat frightening.

A search on the Internet for "advanced humanoid prototypes" or anything along those lines yields unbelievable examples of robots that, were it not for their still synthetic metallic voices and less than human appearance, would be almost indistinguishable from humans in their interactions. In effect, robots are now able to synthesize and understand natural language, so a human can talk to them as they would to another person and they will provide intelligent and coherent answers, and even simulate feelings as well as consciousness.

Robots hold several advantages over us. We can still beat them at some fairly mechanical tasks such as tossing a ball around or tying our shoelaces, but improved heuristic algorithms that take advantage of almost limitless processing power and memory are achieving what seemed impossible just a few years ago. Some of the traits of these robots are quasi-superhuman: enormous and infallible memory, access to all accumulated human knowledge, sensors that memorize every scene and every detail of every minute of every day and that can be tapped into the future, accumulated databases of causes and effects that allow for future predictions, and customized interactions related to every user.

Let's imagine having a robotic assistant, which is no longer a science fiction scenario. These robots, serving as our own personal assistants, would be able to detect our state of mind, emotions, and moods from inflections in our tone of voice, our body language, and our faces, through state-of-the-art sensors that can pick up much more subtle clues than our own conscious senses can do. Based on this accumulated wisdom, these robotic assistants would be able to provide us with information that we need, perform services such as getting cheap tickets for games or the movies, and search for gems of wisdom to assist us, responding to needs that even we ourselves are not fully aware of. These devices exist as prototypes under development, and will slowly but relentlessly find their way into the market until they become an everyday reality.

The implications of these advances in artificial intelligence are too profound to fathom at this point. These future companions that will initially supplement and then even surpass our own capabilities are going to be extremely useful in ways that may improve our quality of life, but at the same time they may threaten the development of our own character and abilities, since they will blur the line between inanimate and living entities. It would not be inconceivable that humans might start developing affection for these contraptions, which will eventually know and be programmed to satisfy our every whim and desire, and will be able to replicate quite easily feelings of friendship and love, all within an intentionally engineered robotic personality that is always going to positively impact our own emotional state. Roboethics is an emerging field, and scientists are slowly starting to seriously consider the implications of how humans relate emotionally to robots. One of my male students once candidly volunteered when I asked him whether he could see himself developing some sort of feeling toward these devices: "If she is pretty, I would fall in love forever."

There are also very important implications when it comes to the collective development of knowledge and the solutions to problems. Futurists refer to "the singularity" as that point in time when artificial intelligence surpasses human intelligence. Once again, the date for this momentous event is arguable and related forecasts uncertain, but it will eventually happen, thus posing humanity with an unprecedented set of challenges as well as opportunities to find solutions to some problems that exceed our human capabilities, from the curing of cancer to accurate weather forecasts.

It will be, indeed, a new world, and the rapid progress of all things related to information processing in the last 20 years is an indication that the scenario may happen sooner rather than later. Students currently in schools will certainly be protagonists in this seemingly unfathomable future within their lifespans, so once again the perennial question looms large in terms of our responsibility as educators: how do we prepare students to live in such a world?

First, we should help our students (and ourselves) become better educated in the inner workings of technological advances, including artificial intelligence. The best way to become an effective user of any technology is to understand how it works, so interaction with the robotic programs available for small children will undoubtedly be beneficial in preparing them to deal with this aspect of reality in the future. Currently, robotics programs are generally held after school hours and are extracurricular, but every student in the school should be exposed at some stage to working with, programming, and learning about the inner workings of robots and artificial intelligence. A true 21st-century curriculum should include not only specific lessons in which technical learning takes place, but also generalized use of robotic assistants as they become available, so that students learn how to best utilize them and develop intuitive capabilities that will greatly help them in their future use of artificially intelligent devices, as well as prepare them for the evolution of those devices.

Ethical Use of Technology

If the above challenges seem difficult, they pale in comparison to what awaits us in terms of developing a curriculum that addresses the impact of technology on our everyday lives. This challenge is even more tantalizing because the effects of technology on individuals and society are not completely understood yet. Emerging technologies defy our understanding of personal and social interactions, especially when they take place online, an environment that most adults currently in positions of responsibility in schools have barely scratched the surface of.

Voltaire is credited with saying that "with great power comes great responsibility," and such is the case with many of the new technologies, which place unprecedented power in the hands of users who had only to purchase the device to "earn" that power. It follows, then, that an important part of school curriculum should be directed to students learning responsible and ethical use of technologies that will continue to increase in their power and capabilities.

As with any value or virtue, the first obvious charge to teachers is to model; in this case, teachers must model responsible and ethical use of technology. It cannot be stressed enough how important it is for teachers to model a continuous learning process using technology, but, at the same time, to be exemplary in its use, taking advantage of every opportunity to bring to the forefront discussions that have to do with potential unethical uses and how to stay away from them.

There are several particular challenges that arise from the most common uses of technology in the school context.

Online Behavior

One of the most challenging aspects of the growing use of technology and the proliferation of opportunities to engage in online games, discussions, and other increasingly sophisticated interactive pursuits is how each one of us becomes an online person that coexists with our real-life self. The sense of detachment derived from interacting from behind the shield of a computer screen sometimes results in a seemingly incomprehensible difference between a person's actions and attitudes online as compared to the person's interactions in real life.

Without getting into psychological issues that are beyond the scope of our discussion, the somewhat illusory anonymity provided by the Web obviously fosters in computer users, hiding behind their virtual avatars, the inclination to venture into online society far more daringly than they do in the physical world, both because their actions are more difficult to trace back to them, and because the virtual environment distances users from the consequences of their actions.

There are many flagrant temptations to indulge in borderline activities on the Internet, from illegally downloading music and movies to viewing porn and using pirated software. The apparent lack of consequences can lure even the most sanctimonious of users into breaking the rules. Ethics and morals notwithstanding, and reserving any value judgments, the role of the school in this context is very clear: there must be very clear rules within the school environment that do not allow for any online misconduct, and the school must set a positive example by using software that has been purchased legally.

This goes far beyond the "acceptable Internet use agreement" that parents have to sign, painstakingly written to try to cover every possible violation. Having such a document is of great value and is a good practice that should be enforced in every school, but in addition to that a positive technology culture needs to be nurtured and fostered at the school.

Social recluses in real life always get pointed out, and it is a legitimate cause for concern when a student is isolated in any manner. Should it be also a cause for worry when students are ostracized online? There is a long way to go in building an accumulated body of knowledge related to this matter, but it surely cannot be ignored any longer, and any well-intentioned efforts by educators will make a big difference.

As with most of the challenges surrounding 21st-century education, there is no direct or simple answer of how to go about this. What is required is the development of an ethical mindset and an accompanying set of values that specifically addresses the fact that our online personalities should not be disassociated from our real personalities. Reflection exercises about this topic that raise the level of awareness of students from a very early age are always a good idea; developing internal reflexes can come to students' rescue when they have to make decisions without the presence of a teacher or family member to guide them.

We already understand how important it is to develop a solid and healthy set of values that form children's personalities from a very early age; we need to place equal importance on the analysis and careful evaluation of students' online lives. In the same way that values, traits, and virtues are fostered through activities in the physical world that are carefully designed to target healthy developmental processes, online activities designed to engender those same values should be embedded naturally within the learning process throughout school.

Encouraging students to be active in the online world and, at the same time, holding them accountable for their actions online, is a healthy first step to a more cohesive online/real-life experience. Although it is perhaps less positive in its approach, another effective strategy for impressing upon students the need to behave online is to remind them of the laws, rules, and regulations in effect that can explicitly punish, even with prison, some of the most serious conduct issues related to online life. It is also a good idea to debunk the notion that there is such a thing as anonymity on the Internet by pointing out that through a variety of methods, a person's online actions can effectively be traced back to them.

Copyright and Plagiarism

Copyright infringement and plagiarism have become increasingly problematic when students are completing assignments that require online research. There is an abundant body of literature dedicated to the topic, as well as tools that assist educators in the ever-more-difficult task of discerning whether student assignments are totally or partially copied. Several Web services, such as Turnitin, will check submitted texts for passages that are not the original work of the students.

However, there is more to learn about digital copyright than the rules about pasting material from Internet sites into assignments. The key skill to be learned is how to tap into the limitless wealth of information available on the Internet without violating copyrights; students must learn to cite sources in the appropriate style. It is very important for the facilitator to model such behavior when conducting the class. It is imperative that teachers painstakingly cite every single one of the sources that they utilize for class explanations or discussions, and that they do the same when giving students references to study. Emphasis should also be placed on the appropriate citing of sources during the correction of assignments.

The key to solving the problem is to formulate our assessment instruments in such a way that they cannot be completed successfully simply by plagiarizing, and that they require original and creative work on the part of the students. Within the "open book" scenario that the Internet places before us, evaluating students on assignments that they can partially or totally copy off the Internet is an unforgivable anachronism. Even though creating such assessments may prove to be much harder than writing the usual factual recall questions, schools should be a testing ground for the real-life workplace, where employees will have access to the Internet but will be challenged to perform tasks that cannot simply be completed by looking them up on the Web.

Hacking

In this era, no school curriculum can afford to ignore issues related to hacking. Hackers have been stealthy companions of the computer revolution, and their jabs at the corporate establishment have captivated the imagination of the public ever since stories started emerging about quasi-legendary exploits conducted at the expense of big companies.

A Puritan approach to the subject that dismisses hacking as an intrinsically evil activity will never resonate with students, who will likely be attracted to anything that defies authority and the accepted rules. In the same way that every school curriculum includes references to contemporary history so that students understand the geopolitical forces that shape society, it is absolutely essential that students be exposed to the history of hacking—the perpetrators' origins, motives, and problems with the law—so that they will become more aware of the ethical and moral issues at stake, and the risks and dangers involved in what students often regard as just a playful activity.

Learning the technical issues related to hacking can serve as the best first step in protecting oneself against such attacks. It is also a good idea to impress upon students the importance of obtaining information from a reliable source and not through unfiltered self-exploration on the Internet, which can lead students down some of the darker online alleys that can be very inviting to adventurous teenagers. It would be advisable to include as part of any technology literacy curriculum an in-depth review of hacking techniques, security measures against hacking, and other technical information related to hacking.

Frank discussions about the hacking movement and its implications and impact on society can provide a healthy dose of awareness and can encourage better discernment in the future. Again, dismissing hackers as malignant outliers is a simplistic stance that would never get past the first layer of skepticism that is innate to students from middle school onward. It is essential that students understand that hacking is an unlawful activity when it implies breaking into networks, obtaining unauthorized passwords, and any other illegal activities designed to gain information to help in hacking exploits. And students also need to understand that what may seem like a harmless adventurous exploration may very well land them in jail.

The other dimension of hacking—hacking with the objective of gaining further technical knowledge—should also be referred to. It is acceptable to channel one's creative energies into trying to make devices go beyond their proffered capabilities, as happened in the early days of computers, when hackers were partly responsible for the revolution that led to the creation of the personal computer. At a time in which there is a widespread proliferation of do-it-yourself, user-uploaded YouTube videos that encourage owners of various devices, most notably cell phones, to attempt to "root" them—that is, break into their operating systems—it is more important than ever that students clearly understand their technological rights and limitations.

Learning about hacking in all of its dimensions is not a difficult challenge in itself, since students are very interested in the topic and, as such, quite motivated to learn about it, and there are abundant online resources that can provide lesson plans, strategies, and references for every age group. The key is that we intentionally include these topics in the curriculum; it is not so important how we do it.

Digital Citizenship

A neglected topic that is intrinsic to the technology revolution is how we can go about becoming digital citizens, what our new duties and responsibilities will be as digital citizens, and how our roles are evolving in the knowledge society.

It is widely acknowledged that in order to become responsible citizens and contribute actively to society, students need to acquire a series of character traits and virtues, and schools invest substantial amounts of money and energy in making available programs, many of which take place after school hours, that are specifically targeted toward learning and exercising those skills, traits, and values. The importance of extracurricular activities, community service, service learning trips, and many other such programs is unquestionable, and those pursuits add value to the school program. The goal is to attempt to provide students with ample experiences that expose them to social interactions, to help them develop empathy and care for others, and, in general, to make them more aware of their roles as active contributors to society.

Somewhat inexplicably, even with the widespread proliferation of opportunities to live our lives online and the acknowledgment that 21st-century society is built upon the sharing of collective knowledge by people all over the world via the Internet, there are almost no efforts to analyze how students can learn to become digital citizens, and almost no activities that address the development of related virtues and values.

The basic principle upon which the knowledge era has been built is the readily available and nearly infinite sources of information that individuals and organizations are placing on the Web at a pace that increases exponentially. Peer-to-peer learning, another fundamental tenet of 21st-century education, depends on the goodwill of individuals who go online to answer questions from their fellow netizens on online forums or other Web-accessible repositories of information, more often than not grouped by thematic interests. Whether you are trying to find out how to advance in a video game, how to solve a computer glitch, or how to tile your bathroom floor, often these groups are a reliable and trustworthy source of information that can be even more helpful than academic sources.

Another more recent but no less important development in the online world is that of consumer reviews as the primary source for gauging the quality of any good or service. Used to find the best and most reasonably priced hotel at a travel destination, to determine which blender purees the best and lasts the longest, and even to find out which local plumber is the most honest and reliable, consumer ratings and reviews are extremely helpful not only in guiding consumers as to the virtues and pitfalls of products but also in providing a measure of accountability for suppliers that has raised the bar in terms of standards, product quality, and customer service. A major problem reported on the Internet and verified to be true can literally cause the bankruptcy of a company or irreversibly damage the reputation of a product.

By sheer force of numbers, the knowledge society sustains itself even though there are far more users who benefit from the Internet than actually contribute actively to expanding the body of knowledge it holds. But there is a significant moral imperative in the current era; we have a certain ethical obligation to not just be Web lurkers and Internet parasites, but rather to add our grain of sand—our bit of knowledge—to the collective, in the same way that our teachers say that we should feel compelled to contribute in the real world.

Here are some possible ways to help shape these traits and virtues in the educational environment:

- **Openness.** Traditionally, when "good" students allow "bad" students to copy their work, it is a moral tragedy of Shakespearean proportions. High morals and discipline standards require that offender and accomplice be punished equally, thus teaching them a very valuable lesson: protect your intellectual property at all times and do not share your capacities and abilities. Even though this is an oversimplification, and even though there are grounds for not allowing students to get by without any effort of their own just by profiting from other people's work, we need to rethink the way we design and structure assignments so that it is done in a way that actually encourages students to share their work as a model for the open society in which we want them to thrive. There is a fine unresolved line between intellectual property and openness, but in the nonprofit and supposedly selfless environment of school it needs to be impressed upon students from a very early age that sharing the products of your efforts is good and not bad. As administrators can commonly attest, their best attempts at building professional learning communities in schools stumble upon the roadblock of teachers who are explicitly and unashamedly unwilling to share their lesson plans and resources with their fellow staff members. Building a culture of openness from the ground up is a must in any 21st-century environment.

- **Publishing on the Web.** In the same way that we encourage students to speak out and be vocal about their opinions and ideas and provide ways for them to showcase their work, we should encourage them to publish on the Web whatever it is that they feel they can contribute to the world in terms of knowledge. If the student has done an exceptionally good classroom project, or is particularly knowledgeable about a certain topic, it is a good idea to encourage them to create a Web site or blog, or to upload videos to social media platforms, or to host discussion groups where they can share their knowledge and make it available to their fellow students via the Internet.

• **Reviews.** Many adults can relate to that guilty feeling you get when you receive an e-mail shortly after purchasing a good or service in which the vendor asks you to post an objective review and rate your user experience, but you know you will procrastinate and never actually get around to doing it. It is highly probable that we have relied on the opinions of previous users or consumers when deciding to buy a product or stay at a hotel. It makes a lot of sense to attempt to ingrain deeply in the inner consciousness of students that it is almost an ethical obligation to post an objective review when we consume something if it is of the nature of product or service that would greatly benefit from users' opinions (i.e., it doesn't seem necessary to have to record our experience using a certain brand of toothpaste or a popular soda drink). And to do this, we must model this behavior ourselves. A very effective strategy would be to let our students know, implicitly or explicitly, when we post reviews that we think are going to be helpful to our fellow consumers. It would not be unthinkable to design a system by which students are held accountable for such posts, and, for example, were required to send links to those posts to their teachers periodically.

• **Help in Online Forums.** We have already made reference to the importance of peer-to-peer learning, both in online forums or in YouTube videos and tutorials that users post to assist others in performing certain tasks to solve specific problems. Since it is unusual to seek the solution to any glitch, malfunction, or question and fail to find it in an online forum or discussion group, one wonders what motivates some Internet users to spend their time regularly checking these peer communities to see if they can assist a kindred soul in distress, when sometimes they are not even thanked for their efforts. The truth is that the staggering number of people that are connected to the Internet accounts for the fact that the vast majority of Internet users are passively benefiting from the wealth of knowledge amassed by a small fraction of good-hearted and generous users who volunteer their time and expertise. Just as we encourage our students to engage in service activities and give of their free time and knowledge to help people in need, we should also communicate clear expectations that they regularly spend time assisting their fellow netizens in online communities by sharing their knowledge and expertise on topics on which they are knowledgeable, even if the scope of their expertise is limited to video games. In particular, many of our young students are very knowledgeable about many things related to technology, and would not find it very difficult to provide some basic tech support to the still very large number of people who find it daunting to come to terms with technological devices. Teachers or mentors could request that students periodically send them information about when they exercise this virtual generosity, so that they can check on the progress and development of such values.

The above list is not intended to be a taxonomy of cyber virtues to be developed; the concepts can be rephrased in any way that makes sense within the current situation in schools and on the Internet. The online world will dynamically evolve, and as the degree of immersion, realism, sophistication, and attractiveness of Web resources increases, the activities of contributing digital citizens will have to improve accordingly.

Privacy

One of the greatest concerns related to the growing use of the Internet is the threat it poses to privacy, as we spend increasing amounts of time online and widen our digital footprints. The proliferation of social media, which has resulted in a semipublic display of many people's private lives, has opened up a level of unprecedented chaos in terms of what we reveal about ourselves on the Internet, and leaves an almost indelible record of our lives for curious eyes to pry open.

In a way, the fact that in the space of a few years our lives have passed from being private to almost automatically public can be reassuring in its merciless authenticity. It is relatively easy to spot people's past transgressions, and to find opinions and acts that may reveal very profound insights about their character, but at the same time, everyone is especially vulnerable to defamation: the spreading of false rumors, ill-intentioned pranks, or any other form of online harassment that could irreparably damage a person's reputation.

There is no universal answer about how to deal with the fact that our lives are out there for everybody to see, as if we were all protagonists of a Big Brother reality show. But a good first step is increasing awareness. Students need to learn how Web sites track their habits through cookies, how search engines customize their preferences in order to return results that are more likely to favor the ads that the search engines will be placing, and how sophisticated and expensive algorithms are being used by firms currently to try to understand social media and consumer habits, all for the sake of increasing sales and becoming more efficient in their marketing efforts. For proof of this,

I suggest that you do a Google search for the phrase "how Target found out a teen girl was pregnant before her father did." Target is one of many companies that employ computer software to try to predict spending habits and make all of us more vulnerable to their marketing ploys. The story is an eye-opening example of the breathtaking power of these predictive algorithms, and the title alone is enough to make most students snap to attention.

Another interesting exercise is to search for "who Google thinks I am," which returns articles that link to the privacy settings in Google, which in turn will yield fascinating information about how, by tracking your Web activity, Google has inferred your age, social status, race, and the topics you are interested in. Most of the time the accuracy of this predictive algorithm is uncanny.

Resorting to extreme "no Facebook" measures to protect one's privacy does not seem like a practical suggestion; we need to accept that social media are an irresistible attraction to many people and specifically to teenagers, who will often find a way to continue relating with their friends through that medium even if they are temporarily banned from it. It makes no sense to resist forces that are beyond our power to control, and social media is definitely one of them. Even though there is no way to come up with a bulletproof privacy insurance policy, openly discussing these issues, not just as a casual conversation whenever the opportunity arises but rather as an instructional topic that forms part of the explicit school curriculum, is the best and safest way to help students deal with them.

A Better Future

I hope that I have not painted such a bleak picture of the future that you are left with the feeling that the magnitude of the challenge before us is too vast and all-consuming to even be worth attempting. The truth is quite the opposite. The fact that most of these problems are open ended and have no single right answer gives us the opportunity to focus on the principles, values, and profound general virtues that can be the best response to this overwhelmingly complex scenario. Yes, technology presents us with a daunting pace of change, and we will be forever caught in the maelstrom of emerging technologies and new advances and will be hard pressed to understand the present technologies, let alone predict those of the future. However, although there are many threats posed by the new technologies, there is also great promise for the future. The possibility of seamless collaboration, of coupling our intelligence with artificial intelligence, of using computer software that is every day more advanced and more connected with our own efforts can result in improved quality of living and solutions to many of the problems that have assailed humans throughout history. Advances in telecommunications have made it more and more difficult to lie to people to keep them "in their place," and have given voice and power to the masses, even more than the invention of the printing press.

Market forces will not humanize technology. As usual, it is up to educators to make sense of the world around us and to decode it in such a way that provides for the healthy development of our students. But we must do it systematically and scientifically, with a conscious and intentional effort to develop a 21st-century curriculum that boldly deals with these challenges within an environment of perpetual uncertainty and change. We cannot leave this important task to haphazard learning that may or may not take place during informal interactions.

CHAPTER FIVE

Content
and Standards

The first step in determining any school curriculum is to decide what content needs to be taught. Every country and school system has a different way of dealing with this fundamental question regarding the planning of formal schooling, and it is generally a much-contested issue that results in profound academic debates and endless arguments and counterarguments over the merits and shortfalls of the system chosen, and the lists of content and standards that are drawn up.

On what grounds is content chosen for a school curriculum that is to be studied by every student in the school system? There are many answers to this open-ended question, but most teachers who have been in the classroom for many years would be hard pressed to come up with any answer other than the obvious one: that content and skills are mostly dictated by a curriculum that has been shaped over the years as a result of many forces, responding to official requirements, the preferences of school administrators and board members, and the ever-more-influential standardized tests.

Content choices can ultimately be traced back to what curriculum planners originally thought would be useful in order to better educate the students who would go through that school system. In terms of the skills and knowledge required to function in the real world, policymakers and educational experts would choose the subjects, sequences, included content, and related skills in order to provide what would be considered a good educational foundation for all students.

Accountability

Closely related to the content included in the school curriculum is the concept of accountability and standards. Regardless of more formal definitions, schools should guarantee that students learn certain content and demonstrate a skill set that constitutes the minimum threshold in order to graduate from whatever stage of the school system is in question. In particular, exit requirements for high school were carefully defined and gave birth to the much-maligned educational standards.

The intention behind standards is a good one: to ensure that all schools will deliver a minimum set of skills and content that guarantee that any student graduating from high school will be in possession of enough tools to perform well in further studies or in the workplace. In the pre-Internet era, with a fixed model of knowledge, that scheme seemed to fit in well with the existing knowledge paradigm, given that outcomes for educational success could be relatively well defined.

The changing and dynamic environment of the 21st century, with a redefined knowledge paradigm and its intrinsically chaotic set of circumstances, however, does not adapt itself well to the world of standardization, fixed content, and universal outcomes for every student in every school system. Among the greatest realizations relating to 21st-century education are that there are multiple paths to success, that outcomes cannot be precisely defined, and that the skills to be acquired will change, that the ultimate goal of the school system is not to fill empty student vessels with knowledge but rather to prepare students and motivate them for lifelong learning, and that each student has a different learning style and different cognitive abilities, and it is the unenviable task of teachers and the school to find, in Michelangelo's words, "the angel in the stone," so as to unleash the potential in each and every child under our charge.

If we look at curriculum through this new prism, the challenges manifest themselves with alarming clarity. Since lifelong learning is the ultimate goal and achieving it requires mostly targeting certain skills and igniting the flame of curiosity and the desire to learn in students, defining a curriculum—the subjects to teach and their relative importance—suddenly becomes a totally different problem altogether. Skills would take precedence over content, and the subjects would be chosen in terms of their ability to foster the learning of skills and not the other way around.

Content Threshold

Even as we recognize the importance of skills over content, and the need for our students to learn new higher-order skills, we cannot think that students should become purely conduits for information that is only looked up online when needed and not permanently stored in the students' brains at all.

Although the Internet will become a natural extension of our brains and information will be seamlessly accessible wherever and whenever we need it, there is still a certain foundation of content knowledge that students need to remember so that they can become not only functional citizens but also cultured individuals that can make decisions without having to check the Internet every time.

Cultural Foundation. What makes for a cultured citizen: a person who is able to function in everyday life, who can understand the world, and who can engage in meaningful interactions with fellow citizens? How much needs to be remembered and about which particular subjects, so that people can function at proficient levels when accessing the Internet? What would be the cultural platform that every student should acquire in order to be well informed? Basing a curriculum on the answers to these questions is common sense, but might seem counterintuitive. Attempting to provide answers for these questions is an interesting exercise, since it instigates a reflection process about what is really important in terms of the culture: is it more useful to remember the dates of a certain historical event or to understand the underlying political causes, economic implications, and long-lasting impact of that event? Revising curriculum under this lens not only will yield some interesting conclusions about what content is important, but also will constitute a very valuable exercise in re-examining our own belief system regarding what it means to be cultured, with the spinoff benefit of reinforcing our local identity and cultural awareness.

Independence from the Internet. Although the Internet will constitute an even more undetectable prolonged intelligence, memory, and consciousness, we can assume that even in the future, functional human beings should not need to access their cell phones or other miniaturized Internet-connected devices to perform everyday acts proficiently. Acknowledging that nearly infinite information is just a few clicks away, decisions will have to be made about what needs to be learned and remembered without having to access online information. If we look at school curriculum through this lens, we will find that many of the concepts that are included may well be done away with, freeing up very valuable time for learning more important stuff or developing and practicing 21st-century skills. The concept of opportunity cost is one of the often most overlooked ideas in education. Opportunity cost is a measure of what we lose when we choose the best alternative over the second-best alternative. If we can remove even a few topics from extensive school curricula, we may find that the time we gain, which we can dedicate to some of the seemingly impossible tasks required by the 21st-century challenge, might outweigh the benefits of teaching more topics.

Platform for Higher-Order Skills. Some of the skills that need to be learned, such as filtering overwhelming amounts of information and discerning which sources are relevant, critical thinking, and metacognition, are higher-order thinking skills that require a certain level of academic sophistication. Content and skills within the school curriculum need to be reassessed in terms of how they provide a platform for higher-order thinking and how they help to develop lower-order thinking skills that will be subsequently used to leverage more complex thinking patterns. Again, it is important to determine which disciplines, subjects, and topics will best target the development of the skills required.

As tempting as it might be to try to find one right answer, there is no magic bullet that will provide for the needs of students universally across school systems all over the world. There is very little literature that provides clear information about epistemology—the nature and scope of knowledge—or on how different subjects will contribute to the learning of certain skills. But a well-intentioned effort to attempt to determine which content is most suitable to foster the development of 21st-century skills and provide an adequate knowledge base would be much better than just continuing to teach the same curriculum as we taught in the pre-Internet era.

The Hierarchy of Subjects

The allocation of hours for the learning of each subject that makes up the school curriculum from kindergarten to high school is what determines their relative importance and how much gets learned about them.

Subjects that relate to literacy, reading and writing, and mathematics have traditionally dominated the curriculum and received a far greater allocation in terms of hours of instruction. Those subjects served students well in the 20th century, when reading and writing were the exclusive means for communication and mathematics not only developed in students certain specific abilities to compute and calculate but also fostered the acquisition of analytical skills.

In the 21st century, with its intrinsic uncertainty, abundant data, fast-paced changes, and a confusingly dynamic environment, and with the explosion of multimedia as the primary means of communication, we suddenly find that those subjects, though well intentioned in their objectives, are ill-equipped to cultivate the adequate development of some 21st-century skills.

Subjects that were traditionally relegated to the status of electives and extracurricular activities, such as art, are acquiring a newfound relevance as experts discover in them opportunities for the learning of more holistic skills that are more in tune with the new knowledge paradigm. I do not dispute the well-deserved preeminence of reading and writing, but it is no longer the predominant medium for communication, and regardless of our value judgments, our students will be consuming increasing amounts of multimedia not only while they are young but also in their time as productive adults in the workplace. They will not necessarily have to write lengthy essays as part of their jobs, but they will almost certainly have to repeatedly create and deliver oral presentations backed up by multimedia support.

In that context, a complete reassessment of the hierarchy of subjects is called for. This has huge implications for school curriculum, staffing, and allocation of time and resources, which may paralyze even the boldest of administrators, who will have to make difficult decisions about those issues. Reforming a school curriculum is hard enough; starting from a blank slate is nearly unthinkable.

Even without rewriting the whole curriculum, some changes can be made in terms of the allocation of the hours dedicated to each subject, especially at the high school level, where there is a certain degree of flexibility and schools have more freedom to shape the curriculum.

A helpful exercise is to make a list of the desired 21st-century skills and then compare that list with a list of the subjects regularly learned at school, ranking the subjects in order of importance based on how well they are likely to cultivate the learning of the skills. I have done this exercise with teachers and administrators from very diverse school settings and grade levels, and its ability to foster very profound curriculum discussions debating the relative merits of each subject and how it contributes to the learning of those skills and arguing over relative time allocations for each subject is fascinating to watch.

This is, of course, an extremely delicate issue, since it could ultimately affect the livelihood of staff members whose hours may be increased or decreased depending on the decisions made, but the debate, notoriously absent from most current educational thinking, is absolutely essential as a first step to updating the curriculum, even if some of the conclusions can only be gradually implemented over time. At the very least it constitutes a first step in the right direction and a testament to the forward thinking of the school leadership.

Standards in the 21st Century

The push to standardization has been synonymous with education in the early 21st century. Standardized tests, international examinations, and other objective measurements of student performance have become the name of the game for assessing educational quality and, mostly through a very linear reward and punishment model, have driven the instructional process by compelling teachers to comply with the required improvement in scores.

While this was happening, progressively bolder and louder protests were raised by educators who saw the futility of the efforts and the intrinsically flawed proposition that all students should perform in the same way at the same point in time, and should be evaluated the same way and be expected to produce the same outcomes.

In her book *The Death and Life of the Great American School System: How Testing and Choice Are Undermining Education* (2010), former U.S. assistant secretary for education Diane Ravitch, a very respected and influential educational leader, candidly reflects on her changed stance with regard to standardized testing and its effect in schools:

> Our schools will not improve if we value only what tests measure. The tests we have now provide useful information about students' progress in reading and mathematics, but they cannot measure what matters most in education. Not everything that matters can be quantified. What is tested may ultimately be less important than what is untested, such as a student's

ability to seek alternative explanations, to raise questions, to pursue knowledge on his own, and to think differently.

The idea of standardized outcomes, rigid testing, and the other accompanying characteristics of the standards movement are clearly not suited to provide a measure of accountability for the 21st century. To start with, we now widely accept that no two students will learn the same way, and that it is the job of the educational system to provide pathways for them to rise up to their full potential, catering to each student's learning abilities and cognitive styles. Additionally, we now realize that individual accountability should be superseded by group or team accountability, since learning is a collective experience and a collaborative venture.

We also now know better than to base our final judgment of the success of the educational process entirely on a summative final assessment that is delivered at the end of the learning with no chance for retesting and that is uniform in its expectations. However, despite this awareness, standards are still considered important. Larry Cuban wrote a seminal paper in 1993 on the introduction of computers in education titled "Computers Meet Classroom: Classroom Wins." Twenty years later, we are facing a similar situation—standards meet the 21st century: standards win. Even though we recognize that the carrots-and-sticks model falls flat in the face of needing to foster intrinsic motivation as the fuel for lifelong learning, educational institutions still largely rely on standards to gauge their success, partly due to the lack of an alternative method.

How would standards look in the 21st-century educational model? To start with, we need to consider the paradox of "nonstandardized standards," since we are trying to juxtapose the idea of a customized curriculum with the need to be accountable for the learning outcomes of every student. Exit requirements for each stage in school would entail that the student is able to demonstrate proficiency at certain skills and tasks, has acquired the level of knowledge and content that is required for successful citizenship, and that they demonstrate the virtues and values that allow them to contribute effectively and genuinely to the team, for starters.

Such objectives cannot be assessed by a sit-down written summative test at the end of school, and would need to be gauged progressively over an extended period of time comprising the school years, in a nonsequential form that allows students to repeat attempts at completing those stages until they have learned enough or are mature enough to be successful.

Such a model of overall school accountability may seem a little far-fetched at this time, and there are obvious implications and complications in terms of the organization of schools, which should be rethought completely to allow for a more organic pathway for students as opposed to the carefully laid out sequential plans with strict time frames that exist today. The heavily grades-based culture that has been dominant for so long in schools should yield to a more holistic assessment system, with personalized feedback from the facilitators/ teachers, who would act more as guides than judges of performance.

All of this may look like a softer, more "new age" version of our current education system. However, the real challenge is to approach the creation of a school accountability model in a scientific and methodical way. Any new, updated plan to account for students' progress will not necessarily be easier or devoid of situations in which students have to overcome difficulties, deal with frustration, negotiate a steep learning curve, etc. Unfortunately, similar attempts to create a less rigid system of education have been labeled as nonrigorous or lacking in educational quality, which substantially undermines the credibility of 21st-century curriculum reform.

Part of the problem is that it will take years for this school of thought to prevail, for the necessary volume of research and practical examples that support this view to be assembled, and for supporters of this education model to gain the political clout needed to overcome the standards movement.

CHAPTER SIX

The 21st-Century Classroom

So far this book has dealt with the general issues that are applicable to learning in the 21st century. Now it is time to take a look at what transpires within the four walls of the classroom.

To start with, the idea that classrooms must have four walls is archaic and contradictory to some of the fundamental tenets of 21st-century education that have been outlined in previous sections. What seems like a perfectly innocent and natural phrase, "what transpires within the four walls of the classroom," is, in itself, describing by virtue of generalization the almost unwitting perpetuation of the old model. The concept of the classroom as the physical space within which learning is delimited in space and time is no longer current; thanks to technology and omnipresent connectivity, learning has become completely ubiquitous and not confined either in location or in time frame to what happens in the "classroom." Advances in telecommunications have essentially obliterated classroom walls, and learning is no longer limited to what the teacher can offer.

This serves to underscore the need to rethink our classroom strategies, and perhaps even to develop a new lexicon for referring to some of the activities that constitute education. The succeeding sections will analyze some general techniques for the implementation of a "21st-century classroom" that build upon the irreversible principles of 21st-century learning.

The Flipped Classroom

One of the few incarnations of 21st-century learning that have become well known is the flipped classroom. This method was fueled by the original and unexpected viral success of Khan Academy, a collection of education videos (initially math related) created by Salman Khan that far transcended its original intent and are now being widely used by students all over the world. The flipped classroom model simply consists of inverting the traditional classroom sequence whereby teachers use physical instructional time in school to lecture and explain, and many student assignments and learning activities occur outside the classroom.

Since the activity of listening to the teacher is passive, and not all students are auditory learners who can understand a concept on their first try, it makes a lot of sense to record lectures and ask students to listen to them ahead of time in the comfort and privacy of their own homes, where they can replay the video as many times as needed in order to better understand the concepts explained. Then, class time can be devoted to cooperative activities and working on assignments, and the teacher can concentrate on guiding those students who need help.

This relative newcomer to the pedagogical arena has many advocates, and its principles are certainly well intentioned, as it attempts to make use of quality time for more personal interactions with students that allow for detailed feedback in the formative assessment process. Implementation of this model in itself is not very complicated at first glance; it only requires that teachers have access to a Web camera and a computer to record their lectures ahead of time and post them online for student viewing. In many cases, the Khan Academy and other sites can even supply already existing videos that can suit the needs of the curriculum unit. There are, however, some issues related to the flipped classroom model that merit discussion.

Level of engagement of students when watching taped lectures. One of the secrets of the Khan Academy's success is not just the concept that it is very appealing to watch videos online at the rhythm and pace every student requires, but also that Salman Khan is a gifted presenter who is engaging even through the often cruel medium of video lectures. His initial videos were quite rudimentary in terms of production, but they came to life through the infectious enthusiasm and clarity of the presenter. How teachers can effectively translate their live explanations into taped videos is, in itself, a formidable challenge that requires substantial training and trial and error before the teachers finds a groove in which they are not only comfortable but also irresistibly engaging. A boring real-life teacher makes for an insufferable taped lecture. Obviously, the proximity and live presence of the teacher in the classroom can clearly help in terms of the level of engagement of students.

The possibility of asking questions. Even though some teachers who are implementing the model are making great efforts to make themselves available online to students after school hours so as to be able to answer questions related to the videos, nothing beats the ages-old clarifying question that students can ask right there in class as soon as it occurs to them. Students who are expected to watch taped lectures at home may need to resort to some independent learning technique like learning from their peers or finding answers online if they get stuck or have a question.

It's a lot of work. The main issue with implementing a fully flipped classroom is that it inescapably entails a lot of work on the part of the teachers. Most teachers that I have spoken with who have attempted to go "full flipped" have acknowledged that if the taped materials have to be renewed for every academic year, it is almost unsustainable in terms of the effort required. Taping a lecture for posterity is far more demanding than just showing up in front of the classroom and explaining a topic to students, an interaction that would be subject to far less scrutiny. Nobody wants to be seen online stumbling over words occasionally, or not always coming across as eloquent and engaging; and it is much harder to be engaging in a video than in real life. One way around this problem is to assume that, once a standard set of explanations, lectures, experiments, and directions are taped, they can be reused for several years. However, given the general conditions we now operate under and the fast-paced changes that are the norm, we may suspect that the life cycle of some canned lectures would be measured more in months than in years.

It still perpetuates the traditional teacher-centered learning model. Even though the flipped classroom is a good attempt at using computers for learning purposes and spending quality time on personal interactions with students, it still heavily accentuates the teacher-centered model; the heart of the experience is still the venerable old teacher lecture. An updated version of the flipped classroom that doesn't rely entirely on lectures taped by the teacher but incorporates materials that are available online, and links to resources that students can avail themselves of in order to learn the topics independently, may be more conducive to the 21st-century learning environment. However, independent learning can take place within the physical space and time frame of formal schooling, with the teacher's role being that of facilitator, mentor, and guide.

Truly interactive materials are hard to produce. Most of us who have either been taped or have attempted to tape ourselves delivering explanations have come to the hard realization that what seems to be a rather straightforward endeavor is actually very difficult, and that even if we think of ourselves as engaging presenters in real life, we might come across as flat and somewhat uninteresting on a video screen with just one camera pointing at us. In order to provide students with a truly interactive experience and extend the possibilities of technology as a medium of delivery, the computer-based component of the flipped classroom should include links to sites that provide tutorials, projects, resources, teacher explanations, screen captures of games, and other resources that far exceed the capabilities of most teachers, who, after all, have degrees and experience in education but probably not in video production, computer programming, and Web design.

The flipped classroom model is undoubtedly a positive attempt to bring down to the level of everyday school practice some of the principles of 21st-century education. However, this model falls into the trap of trying to do old things the new way, which may prove to be even more cumbersome than breaking from the traditional model altogether and going for a full-fledged 21st-century pedagogy.

Blended Learning

There are many definitions of blended learning, but it is not my intent to dwell too much on precisely enunciating the concept but rather to share the underlying principles. The concept of blended learning implies a combination of online and face-to-face learning, with the online component giving the students a measure of control over the pace of the learning process.

Blended learning makes use of learning management system software (Moodle, for example), which handles administrative support of the online portion of the course as well as the structuring of content, activities, evaluations, and other components of the online learning program. In order to make effective use of the possibilities provided by technology and make the remote learning experience more engaging, it would be advisable to try to include as many simulations, games, videos, and interactive pursuits as possible in order to enhance what would otherwise be just a computer-based conversion of the textual learning model. Too often online courses underutilize these possibilities and, as such, are just ill-fated attempts to sustain the old model, but with the addition of technology.

The blended mode of learning has several interesting advantages, especially when the online component is relevant and engaging. The possibility of students using interactive tutorials or simulations to learn the content and skills entailed in that unit of study at their own pace and receiving the kind of instantaneous feedback that is provided by a computer-generated tutorial or gaming experience would undoubtedly help the students who find it difficult to learn in the conventional face-to-face environment where the teacher explains the topic. Also, online courses often allow for a record of student progress, and make students responsible for their own learning in ways that prepare them for the lifelong learning process.

Challenges associated with blended learning have to do with the difficulty of building truly engaging interactive experiences through the learning management system, which takes a lot of effort and time, or finding adequate third-party resources that fulfill that role, such as commercial games, tutorials, or simulations. Teachers also need to learn about managing the blend between physical instruction and the online component so that the learning experience can be more organic and can benefit from both components. This model calls for a totally different approach in terms of structuring the sequencing and the pacing of content and skills, and, as with any new method, many teachers find it hard to move away from linear unit planning and concatenated evaluations.

Another issue is that blended learning needs to allow for students to spend considerable amounts of time either at home or during class accessing the online environment at paces that are not going to be the same for any two students, which has implications for teachers in terms of planning. A blended learning environment is not one where the teacher can resort to saying, "Finish your tutorial for the written test on Friday"; it requires more of a checklist or road map approach, where students would be completing stages in the learning process but not necessarily in a prescribed order or at a given date and time.

Another factor that always looms large whenever introducing technology-rich learning is the fact that not all students are able to immediately thrive within that environment, especially if computer-based learning is a somewhat new innovation in the school. Despite having grown up with technology, not all students find it easy to immediately relate to computer-assisted learning, especially when they are being held accountable for the learning process themselves. For the most part, children and teenagers still use computers mostly for entertainment and communication through the Internet, so the switch to using them for formal learning purposes is not immediate or automatic. And in most schools, the traditional environment predominates, so all that students know about learning is the traditional method. For that reason, it is always advisable to start using blended learning that utilizes technology to provide a richer and more meaningful learning experience from a very early age, and to gradually and progressively expose students to computer-based learning.

Technology Tools for Active Audience Participation

Back in the early years of the 21st century, Dan Gillmor (2004), an American journalist and author of *We the Media,* came up with a great catchphrase to define how learning is no longer a top-down activity where the person presenting is the only one who is knowledgeable. He refers to "the former audience" as a way to indicate that the audience is no longer passive but rather is a protagonist of the learning experience. One of the accepted tenets of 21st-century education is that learning from peers and creating a collective learning community is not only a desirable trait of a 21st-century classroom but also one that will empower and enrich the learning experience by providing greater audience engagement and feedback that would be useful in the learning process.

To this effect, there are some technological tools available that will make audience participation faster, easier, and more personal. Most of the currently available tools that we will outline are based on students sending in answers via their cell phones or Internet-connected devices independently and anonymously. The great value of such tools is that they give an equal voice to everybody, and do not rely on the usual classroom dynamics that favor students who are extroverts, or who exercise leadership in the particular peer-to-peer culture in school. As teachers, we are all too aware of how many students never volunteer answers for fear of being ridiculed, and do not participate actively in class discussions because they are ashamed, shy, or both. Sending in answers anonymously over the Internet not only does away with many common inhibitions, but also allows for a lot of answers in a very short period of time, and answers that are much more candid and sincere than the politically correct type that many students use in their classroom interactions, especially when the teacher is present and the stakes are high in terms of expectations of appropriateness.

I am not suggesting that the use of these tools and electronic devices is the end of the sacrosanct and very beneficial classroom discussion, thus turning students into automatons that can only express themselves through their cell phones. These are just alternative methods to be used occasionally that can be very advantageous to engage the "former audience." Having oral discussions and helping students develop the skills associated with them, as well as providing a venue for socialization, are still very important.

Online Interactive Data Walls

Online interactive data walls are basically Web sites that allow users, via their smart phones or other Internet-connected devices, to beam in short, tweet-like messages that express what they are thinking about a particular topic. Most of these tools now also allow for the uploading of pictures, and the following of hashtags on Twitter and social media as a way to see what is being said in the cyber world about a particular topic relevant to the learning situation. In general, these tools purposely do not allow for the capturing of the responses, which are dynamically displayed on the wall and refreshed continuously so that all messages can be read for only a short period of time.

This tool is ideal for capturing the mood of the audience, for asking audience members to reflect and to express ideas and opinions, and for formulating initial learning objectives as a check-in or check-out activity in any learning scenario. These walls can be seen as a sort of collective stream of consciousness of the room, expressing in a qualitative way how people feel or what they think about a particular topic. Notable examples of this type of tool include Wiffiti and Wallwisher, and it can be expected that new players will appear in the market.

In a traditional classroom situation, this could be used for any of the following applications:

- Students sending in what their learning objectives are for particular unit, what they would wish to learn, and what they think they don't know.

- Students expressing their opinions about a video that they have watched, or a text they have just read.

- Students summing up in one word how they feel about the class.

- As a check-in activity, students expressing what they have done over the weekend, how they're starting the week or the day, or what their expectations are for a lesson.

- Students expressing feelings about the class, such as their greatest fears, their expectations, how they feel about an upcoming test, etc.

- Students expressing their moods by answering a prompt such as "How are you feeling?"

These examples serve to indicate that these walls are ideally suited for capturing moods, feelings, and moments in ways that are transient by nature. Data walls are not as appropriate for more serious academic stuff, such as checking the understanding of the students about a particular topic, or their knowledge of content.

Online Polls

Another great way to capture input from the "former audience" is by using online poll systems. These are basically Web sites that allow users to submit answers to questions posed by the presenters via their cell phones by means of text messages, accessing Web-based links where they can enter their answers, or through their Twitter accounts.

Most of these Web-based services, which in almost all locations offer a free but somewhat limited service allowing only for a limited number of responses and some interactivity and functionality, have the following features:

- Questions can be open ended, multiple choice, and, in some locations, Liekert scale (for instance, grading from 1 to 5 where 1 is very satisfactory and 5 is unsatisfactory) or other more sophisticated choice-based question types.

- Participants can generally view the responses online and in real time, whether by periodically refreshing textual answers submitted by the users or by showing the results of the multiple-choice poll as the answers are entered. In all cases, the presenters may choose not to show the results of the poll so as not to influence the answers that have not yet been submitted.

- Responses can be downloaded to a text file, a spreadsheet, or, in some cases, a PowerPoint presentation. Some other popular options include interfacing directly with word cloud software.

- With some of the sites, profanity filters can also be included so as to make sure that overtly creative partici-pants do not disrupt the experience.

Polls can be started, stopped, and reset as the presenter sees fit, and answers are recorded until the account holder decides to delete them. Setting up these polls is, for the vast majority of such Web sites, very easy and intuitive, as is collating and recording the answers.

Classroom applications of these tools are many and can be very interesting:

- **Check for understanding.** The almost rhetorical query to students, "Do you understand?" that teachers have uttered since time immemorial in classrooms is gener-ally met by acquiescing stares, with students not daring to express their confusion lest they be singled out or risk compromising their grade. But posting questions through online polls that are responded to anonymously by the students genuinely allows for the teacher to gauge how well a lesson is going and if the content and skills are being mastered or not. Since the poll also provides a record, the class can keep track of its own progress and can receive instantaneous feedback on how well they are doing. Open-text questions also give the teachers a good measure of how well students can express and rephrase what they are learning.

- **Allow students to express themselves.** Online polls can give students a collective voice in expressing them-selves about some topic or issue, thus providing a more engaging live link with the audience. There are many topics in the learning environment that allow students to express their feelings, concerns, or ideas, or their take on the subject or on a source they have read; this makes learning a more personal experience that students can more readily relate to. Results can be compiled in a text document, or set up to record whatever it is that the teacher wants to poll the class on, so as to later make it part of the learning experience.

• **Surveys.** Surveys, one of the primary uses of online polls, can also be applied in the classroom setting. When the teacher needs to garner valuable information about students, such as study habits or technology availability, the use of these anonymous surveys can provide invaluable information to be used in reformulating the learning strategies.

• **Collaborative learning.** The learning of 21st-century skills is, by nature, a collaborative effort. One of the great advantages of these online polls is that answers are there for everyone to see, so, when properly designed, activities that utilize these polls can include a peer-to-peer learning dimension. Because students will be seeing the answers as they are constantly refreshed on the screen, and they can also be compiled and sent back to students to assist in their learning, properly formulated questions (not questions that all students would respond to the same way) can significantly contribute to the collective learning experience.

One of the greatest advantages of using online polls is that in a relatively short period of time, a lot of information can be collected, processed, and made available to all involved. Without such a tool, it would be almost impossible to record and report on the ideas, information, knowledge, or opinions of a large group of people.

Every time I go to a conference and spend time in the exhibit hall I find it amazing that companies are still pushing the good old clickers—the calculator-like radio frequency devices that are given to students to enter information via old-time cumbersome key words. These devices, which before these Web-based services were pioneering efforts to achieve similar objectives, are not only expensive but also quite impractical in their use and limited in their scope. Nowadays, most students would have functional cell phones that can perform the same task, not to mention tablets or computers that allow for far more possibilities.

Typepads

One of the relatively new players in the world of tools for group work are online collaborative typepads. These online services comprise a typing pad that users can access concurrently in real time, whilst they can be editing and making changes to the document. Each user has a distinctive color that distinguishes their work in the process and the access to the document in real-time is seamless—anybody can add, modify, and even delete what other users are doing at the time.

The main use of these pads is to put together work that people are doing simultaneously, so it would be ideal for small groups working on an assignment and then pasting their work into a single document that serves as a compilation of what everybody has done.

The really intriguing application of collaborative typepads, and one that is quite relevant in the context of how to help converge the crowd's knowledge into a finite document that harnesses results of the collective learning process, is to have a group of people whose communication is otherwise restricted work on creating a single document that tries to reflect a position or idea over an extended period of time. For example, an interesting classroom exercise would consist of having the whole class work on a collective assignment, such as an exercise that involves analyzing a source, listing causes and effects, or even writing an argumentative essay, with all the students contributing to the same typepad. Since everybody in the class will get the same grade, it will become the quintessential team effort, but will require students to communicate in ways that are nonconventional. The rubric that details how the class will obtain the grade must include participation as a desired outcome—that is, the number of colors, and therefore users, that are reflected in the final document should be as large as possible to reflect that many students have actively taken part in the development of the document. When the groups are somewhat large, a possible variation of this exercise is to work in small groups and have one member of each group accessing the collaborative type-pad and channeling through it the result of their group's interactions.

This being a relatively new application, there isn't much formal research on whether typepads constitute a good conduit for channeling the collective wisdom of crowds, but it is certainly an interesting experiment and also an exercise in online civility.

Word Clouds

Word clouds, most notably through the pioneer application Wordle, have been around for some time and are one of the flashier incarnations of what technology can do in terms of pulling together input from a group of people. Word clouds consist of an interface that receives a text document and then displays the words in some sort of graphical layout such that the words that are most used throughout the document are bigger in size and the ones that are less frequent are smaller.

This is a really interesting way to process input from a large group of people, since words that are used a lot are instantly visualized by virtue of the bigger font size. The collective effect can be quite compelling since, in a nonconventional way, copious amounts of text can be made sense of in terms of the general ideas without the need to read through lengthy feedback. Word clouds are one of the few applications that really utilize technology in a way that is quite relevant to leveraging the processing power of the computer in analyzing text.

Of course, a little bit of editing needs to be done before processing the raw text, so as to condense into single words terms that are almost the same, such as "students" and "student," and to account for spelling mistakes.

Even though the first uses of word clouds were as attractive ways to display text, the real power of the application in an educational setting cannot be underestimated. Even though there is no actual literary analysis of the text and what emerges is simply a graphical representation of the words that are used most often in the writing, it is still a very interesting concept, since the computer is able to highlight trends that perhaps even the writer is not aware of.

Classroom applications of word clouds include:

- Paste a very lengthy external document into word cloud software with the goal of being able to graphically convey the main ideas. An interesting activity would be to ask students to send in via an open-ended text question within an interactive poll what they think the main concepts in a book are, and then compare it with the word cloud that results from analyzing the whole text of the book.

- Create a word cloud out of all of the speeches done by a certain historical figure, which would yield very interesting insights into the themes or topics that were a constant throughout the public life of that person.

- Analyze through word clouds fundamental foundational documents, such as laws or the Constitution.

- Compile all work done by students for certain assignments, if it was handed in in digital form, in order to reflect what the whole class thought were the most important concepts within a topic.

In general, the purpose of word cloud applications is to present text in an attractive way, and also to provide a way to process large amounts of text. Undoubtedly, there will be many more applications in the future that target the analysis of text through computer algorithms, and this first application of that concept is a positive step forward in opening up students' minds to that possibility.

Online Meeting Rooms

Online meeting rooms, such as Live Minutes, are rapidly gaining ground in providing free online platforms for collaboration that integrate text, documents, graphics, and even audio and video. These online meeting spaces will, without doubt, constitute a primary source for professional work in the future, as teams in different locations are able to use them to interact with an increasing degree of transparency and speed and working on a common multimedia project. In that context, it is important that students learn how to use these tools and the associated concepts, and, more importantly, practice successfully collaborating over the Internet in a complex and rich environment that includes different media.

These applications include features that allow participants to receive a digital document that reflects not only the final product but also the process, and, as students have increasing access to connected devices, adopting one of these platforms for collaboration can be an interesting and fruitful proposition for homework, or even class work.

Once again, the skills to be garnered here are not just technical skills related to the use of the application itself, but also collaboration skills within an electronic medium. Assessment rubrics should reflect the process as well as the final product, and teachers can have access to a digital record of how the project was done as a way to gauge contributions by the different team members.

Synchronized Notes

Another increasingly popular networked application is software that allows for collaborative and synchronized sharing of multimedia notes, with increasing levels of complexity and sophistication. These are basically platforms that allow for several users to share a common notebook, which is stored in the cloud and periodically synchronized seamlessly to the user so that it is as updated and current as possible.

These notes applications usually function seamlessly over different devices, such as PCs, Macs, the Apple family of portable devices, Android tablets, smart phones, etc., so that users taking notes on their cell phones would find those same notes on their desktop computers by virtue of the background synchronization of the software.

Classroom applications of these platforms are very direct. The software can be set up so that users share a common notebook, which allows the teacher to seamlessly push whatever is being done in class to student accounts so that they can all see what has been done in class, providing a rapid way of communicating with the students about class assignments, projects, deadlines, etc. Notes taken by the students could also be synchronized, so that everybody in class would have access to what every other student has been doing or the notes they have taken during lessons.

This software has advanced capabilities that allow for the sharing of images, videos, audio, links, and documents that enrich the learning experience and can populate the digital portfolio of learning materials for the class. Lately, this software has also been integrated into online meeting rooms, so that notes taken in them can be brought into online discussions and later saved back to the notebooks for distribution and sharing.

As with any other similarly powerful networked learning application, synchronized note-taking requires carefully defined protocols for editing and sharing, and a certain work ethic shared by the class, since giving editing privileges to every member of the class makes the whole notebook vulnerable to any ill-intentioned modification. The adult learner (a.k.a. the teacher) should provide guidance and structure to students so that the note-taking process does not become more chaotic than it usually is. For example, it is a good idea to organize class work separately from notes taken by students and to establish a way to distinguish student contributions from what the teacher has included in the notes.

Blogging

Blogs are an older but no less relevant application. These familiar and easy-to-create Web sites provide an easy platform for sharing information, tidbits, links, and resources, along with anything else that the blogger might want to publish for the audience. Blogs have been extensively used by teachers to post classroom materials, assignments, and other resources.

When defining a digital model for learning, blogging can be a viable alternative for student expression and the posting of assignments, both because it is an easy to use, freely accessible platform that students can later use in real life, so being trained in blogging would be interesting and valuable to them, and also because the very nature of blogs allows for viewing and commenting by other users, thus embodying one of the main principles of 21st-century learning—collaboration and learning from peers.

There are, of course, multiple platforms for blogging and each has its own distinctive features and characteristics. Some, like Tumblr, allow for multi-user posting, so an unlimited number of participants can contribute and add to the blog. This can be quite an attractive feature when creating a blog that serves as the record of a collective learning experience, since it allows all members of the class to share their knowledge and resources, as well as comment on what others have posted.

Blogs can be used for both compiling all resources and learning activities for the class and serving as a place for students to post their own contributions to the learning experience. The skills required to successfully post to a blog—the selection and filtering of relevant information, synthesizing, analyzing, and summarizing—are all quite relevant in the context of the 21st-century classroom, and they constitute a very good example of using telecommunications for collaboration.

Bridging the Gap Toward Collaboration

Regardless of the tool, the common defining element in all of the technologies mentioned in this chapter is the fact that the teacher no longer holds absolute power in the learning process, and utilizes existing state-of-the-art technology to communicate with students, engage them in interactive exercises that require their contributions, and then analyze the results of those activities to inform and reshape, if necessary, the learning process. Engagement is not the only objective: attempting to move from the divergent thinking of a large group of people through the process of converging toward concrete outcomes that can then form part of the learning is a great exercise to model, since it constitutes a very relevant skill in today's workplace, where leaders need to tap into collective sources of knowledge and wisdom in order to define processes and products.

CHAPTER SEVEN

Learning
21st-Century Skills

In order to function within the knowledge era, students need to learn some completely new skills that will constitute the toolset that will enable them to survive and, hopefully, thrive in the new era. There are countless taxonomies that attempt to artificially constrain and categorize these new, dynamic, and evolving skill sets. Though precisely defining and categorizing these skills is not important, it is essential for schools to foster the development of some new skills that stem from the needs that students will have and the opportunities and infinite possibilities for learning in this globally interconnected, fully searchable world that the Internet places at our fingertips.

Learning these skills requires, in most cases, a new mindset regarding the learning process itself, since, in the usual school scenario, we strive for the acquisition of progressively more advanced skills that are attuned to certain tools, and we work so that our students are able to perform highly sophisticated tasks with those tools. In our new world of intrinsic uncertainty, where every specific tool is ephemeral, we instead need to focus on the principles, and on providing students with skills that are more focused on metacognition so that when content changes and new skills are needed, the foundations for the learning process are deeply embedded in the intuition and reflexes that students have acquired through their formal schooling experience.

Examples from early attempts at technological education provide us with examples of why creating a taxonomy of needed skills won't work. In the early days of technology education, whole subjects and countless hours were dedicated to learning every intricate menu and function of a software package, such as a word processor. Teachers jumping on the technology bandwagon were eager to test their students on the most minute and well-hidden subtlety in a menu, and to have their students memorize commands. Then the students were assessed within conventional sit-down written tests. Now we know that change is the name of the game, and that the cutting-edge software of today is the old relic of tomorrow.

In this era, we should actually give students a very poor grade if we ask them to perform an outrageous task using a word processor and they answer by memorizing shortcuts or menus. The assessment rubrics should instead value going to the Internet, searching for the answer, and then getting it right through trial and error, since that kind of inquiry-based attempt is closer to the heart of the lifelong learning process that schools need to cultivate above all else.

The following sections will outline suggested ideas and strategies to cultivate the learning of core 21st-century skills. The suggestions do not constitute a taxonomy, and are not meant to be an exhaustive list of relevant skills that will be needed in the ever-changing context of the 21st century. But the central skills are here to stay, since they are rooted in the fundamental principles of lifelong learning and therefore transcend even the fast-paced technological changes and new tools to be developed. It would also be pointless to try to come up with step-by-step recipes of how to help students learn the skills, since each classroom context and school setting is very different. Instead, these sections will streamline the main principles and suggest general strategies that can later be adapted to the particular subject matter and age and ability of the students.

Filtering

If there were hypothetical rankings of 21st-century skills in terms of their relevance, undoubtedly filtering would top every one of them.

The most dramatic impact caused by the omnipresence of the Internet and the irreversible infinite accessibility to information is that everybody will have to deal with overwhelming amounts of data that need to be filtered in order to obtain the desired information.

The massive implications of this change in the educational setting cannot be overstated. Whereas in the past the world in which we lived presented us with limited sources of information to choose from—books, journals, and magazines that all implicitly included a careful review process with safeguards that ensured at least a minimum threshold of quality of the stuff that was published—today's world is a playground for knowledge mavericks.

In his very interesting book *The Shallows: What the Internet is Doing To Our Brains* (2011), author Nicholas Carr relates a story that summarizes admirably the quest of learners since time immemorial:

> On the evening of April 18, 1775, Samuel Johnson accompanied his friends James Boswell and Joshua Reynolds on a visit to Richard Owen Cambridge's grand villa on the banks of the Thames outside London. They were shown into the library, where Cambridge was waiting to meet them, and after a brief greeting Johnson darted to the shelves and began silently reading the spines of the volumes arrayed there. "Dr. Johnson," said Cambridge, "it seems odd that one should have such a desire to look at the backs of books." Johnson, Boswell would later recall, "instantly started from his reverie, wheeled about, and replied, 'Sir, the reason is very plain. Knowledge is of two kinds. We know a subject ourselves, or we know where we can find information upon it.'"

We can only lament the plight of learners in the pre-Internet era. They either had to remember things themselves, or have physical access to the limited places where the information could be found, which often involved a significant investment of time and money. With all due respect to the hard-working librarians that have been wonderful in opening worlds of knowledge to people like myself from a very early age, allow me to say that one of the greatest anachronisms of the world today is the system for classifying books in a library, which painstakingly codes them so that they're easier to physically spot on the shelves.

All of the above intends to illustrate the magnitude and the extent of the change that we now enjoy. Whereas in the old model, learners would have to have physical access to knowledge and invest considerable amounts of time and money to come by these resources and then find the information they needed, we just need to pull out our connected devices and search for whatever it is that we need to know. It can be argued that not all content is online yet, but the growth of available online information is a one-way street, and efforts are currently underway to digitalize all existing books. The flip side of that coin is that whenever we search for information, we get more than we bargained for, and much of it has very dubious relevance and authenticity.

Checking the Authenticity of the Source

The first step in the filtering process involves checking the authenticity of the source. Since, again, anybody with access to the Web can at no cost create a Web page and proclaim themselves to be experts on any topic of their choosing, it is essential that students do not naively believe everything they read on the Internet.

Students must be reminded, after deciding that the contents of a Web site are relevant to their search, that they must find out where the page originated. The process involves:

- Finding out who the Web page belongs to.

- Finding out whether the individual or organization that created the site has any particular interest or bias toward the topic. For example, an analysis on the Second World War posted on a neo-Nazi Web site would not be credible.

- If the page has an author, finding the author's biography and affiliation, and whether that author has academic credentials or knowledge of the subject matter in question.

- If the object of the search is to be used for academic purposes, finding out what the vetting processes are for the publication of information on that particular Web site—whether it is peer-reviewed, or if there is some other kind of process in place that ensures that there are filters and checks for the accuracy of the publication.

Their lack of skepticism and a flippant dismissal of the importance of double checking sources combine to make students incredibly naive when it comes to believing the authenticity of sources on the Internet, and vulnerable to being easily duped. Developing their academic instincts in a spoon-fed environment, where teachers have supplied them with healthy doses of invariably correct information, does not help students learn the needed reflexes to spot content that may be biased, ill-intentioned, or simply erroneous.

One of the most common slights in school curricula is believing that the criteria for detecting inauthentic sources will be developed implicitly, since it is never addressed explicitly during the curriculum, and waiting until students get older and/or have access to the Internet to start training them in discerning the validity of sources. It is important to expose students from a very young age to sources that are invalid, and to dispense them regularly during the learning process, and to reward students for correctly detecting them. This involves, every now and then, and without prior warning, including within assignments sources that are initially ridiculously wrong and then eventually more subtly biased or incorrect, or authored by people whose opinions are self-evidently subjective. We need to train our students to be absolutely critical and distrustful of any source that comes their way, and to develop a healthy skepticism that even includes us, their teachers. Nothing is guaranteed. We must prepare them for the unpredictable and reward them when they spot that their formerly trust-worthy adult educator is purposefully throwing them into deep water to see if they swim or sink.

Some examples may include:

- A character in a fairytale that is feeding misinformation to the other characters to gain some sort of advantage in the story. The lesson learned could be how the gullible characters are misguided by not checking the information they received.

- A history text that is directly pasted from some propaganda instrument with clear partisan intentions.

- A purported scientific text that is actually written by some commercial firm in the pharmaceutical industry assigning properties to a drug using language that is vague and misleading.

- Statistical information that is taken out of context to demonstrate a point that is not true.

- An argumentative essay by an author whose ideology is clearly aligned with the purpose of the conclusions in the text.

Developing a finely honed instinctive reflex to spot fishy contents and the ability to sort out relevant information is a very lengthy process that should be worked at intentionally throughout the years in the formal schooling process. This should not be a happenstance occurrence; opportunities to develop this skill should be infused throughout all subjects and from a very early age.

Constructing Successive Queries

Another assumption that educators frequently make is that students will learn how to search the Internet on their own. Even though look-ing for information has become increasingly simpler, thanks to new capabilities and the customization of the user experience sought by search engines, and the fact that it has become a fairly intuitive process, it is simply unbelievable that such a crucial skill—the one skill that will open up the doors of the world of infinite knowledge— is generally not taught systematically and intentionally in schools.

Finding information on the Internet is a process that often starts with a somewhat limited initial knowledge of the topic, and continues through successive stages that refine the search and converge on the answers required. We all know certain people who are "search gurus"—individuals who are called upon to find what other people cannot find on the Internet and who seem to work some sort of black magic to find things others cannot. The palpable glow of satisfaction such masters display when they hit the online jackpot is not the result of a secret supernatural search engine but rather of skills that can be learned and perfected over time.

Even though there is no way to generalize and account for every possible search process, and the steps to gather information will greatly depend on the nature of the search involved, the general pro- cedure can be broken down into a series of suggested stages so that gradually Internet users become more efficient at actually finding what they are seeking.

- **Initial uneducated general search.** This first stage in- volves having a general idea of what it is that needs to be found but not necessarily knowing the proper termi- nology or the keys to a successful search for the topic. In this initial search, the clear objective is to familiarize ourselves with the topic and try to find details that will eventually help refine the search process. Within this first part, for example, when the objective is to gain a lit- tle education on the topic, Wikipedia or blogs would be acceptable sources as a first-stop quick resource to gar- ner some general knowledge. It is not so important in this initial part of the process to be very punctilious about the accuracy of the Web site. The idea is to learn a bit more about the topic so as to be able to continue in the search process, not to utilize these results as the end product of our search.

- **Narrowing down of the search terms.** The first stage would ideally yield certain terms that we can try to search for in order to gain the information that we are trying to find. This second stage in the process involves trying out searches with the keywords that were obtained in the initial stage and seeing how each of them can or cannot guide us to our desired results. The aim of this funneling stage is to definitively converge toward a narrowed down set of results. It is not so important here to analyze the results, but rather to come up with the final construction of the query itself that will best take us to the concepts sought.

- **Final search.** The last stage of the process generally occurs once the user is aware of which search terms will get the desired results. With the query refined, this stage involves finding the most relevant and trusted sources to be used as the end product of the search. It should be noted that, for efficiency's sake, the thorough analysis and discernment of the validity of each source is reserved for this latter stage, since it is only here that we will be using the results for our learning purposes.

Educators are very aware of the need to teach study skills, and we go to great efforts to help students develop study habits such as synthesizing, summarizing, and taking notes, which serve them well in the conventional brick-and-mortar environment. In the same way, learning how to construct a search query should be an essential skill that needs to be learned successively, by developing battle-tested methods and procedures, running case studies, and guiding students to obtaining good results.

For instance, exercises can be devised so that students have to search for a deliberately vague topic and gradually move toward more concrete answers. One example that I sometimes use is the search for extraterrestrial life. I tell students I want them to find out as much as they can about the possibilities of extraterrestrial life. This is a great topic, because it is not only vague but also plagued by many outrageous sources of information that refer to UFO sightings and little green men. Students should narrow down the scope of the topic—that is, move from the bizarre and ridiculous ideas about aliens and UFOs to scientific conjectures that there could be microbial life on Mars and some of Jupiter's moons, and finally summarizing the state-of-the-art current information on the topic from objective sources that are research based and not fueled by speculation.

Helping students adopt an educated methodology for searching is one of the best things an educator can do for them. Not having a formal process in place that fosters the learning of searching skills is one of the biggest shortcomings of our education system.

Learning How to Filter Excessive Data

A very important dimension of the filtering process has to do with how to deal with overwhelmingly abundant data that cannot be processed analytically. Although we delight in the wonderful blank check that we have been handed that gives us access to nearly all accumulated human knowledge, wading through unlimited amounts of information can be confusing and staggering.

We cannot expect our students to cope with this infinite data scenario on their own, and to develop the skills needed to process and see through staggering amounts of information automatically. These skills need to be learned progressively from a very early age and with increasing levels of complexity as students get older.

This particular part of the "learning how to filter" process is aggravated by the fact that school has always been an artificially protected environment when it comes to data. Irrespective of the topic and the age level, almost the entirety of school assignments and assessments are immaculately efficient in their handling of data. Whenever solving a problem or looking for sources to answer questions, students are generally given precisely as much data as they need—not one item more, not one item less. This is even more evident in math and science, where problem solving is treated as a self-defined minimalistic art: when students are trying to solve a problem that has more data than needed, hands shoot up immediately, and students ask: Why are you giving us this information? How are we supposed to use it?

Learning to deal with overabundant data does not necessarily have to be a computer-related activity and does not require access to technology. It is more about developing a mindset that whenever presented with information, the first step toward solving a problem is discerning which information is needed, or relevant, or useful for successfully completing the task.

This requires educators to make a conscious effort to expose students, from a very early age and at the level of difficulty that they can handle, to more data than they need as the norm, and not the exception. It may be argued that presenting students with excessive data can be confusing and that the reason assessments have evolved to contain only as much data as is needed is to help students develop the mental skills required for those particular processes without adding an element of distraction. I am not advocating that the learning process should be chaotic from day one. However, as much as possible, when students are mature enough to understand the issues at stake and be able to solve problems, a final layer of complexity should be added so that they learn to handle more data than is necessary for successful completion of the task at hand.

Possible examples of how to incorporate overabundant data include:

- In mathematics or science exercises, include more data points than are needed to solve the problems. Part of the task of students would be to discern which of the items supplied are the ones that are relevant to the question.

• Also in math and science, include data that are clearly out of range—measurements and values that are self-evidently wrong—and reward students when they detect and discard them.

• When doing an assignment in social sciences that is based on reading different sources and then answering questions, train students in selecting from a variety of sources, not all of which need to be used in solving the exercise, and using only the ones that are most appropriate for the problem at hand.

• In early childhood, when setting up a task to be performed, train children to sort out and select what they need to complete that particular task, letting them know ahead of time that they need to use as few materials as possible. For instance, if they are using wooden blocks to build a particular shape, even if it takes longer, have them take the shapes from a box that contains all different shapes, including several that are not needed for that particular model. In terms of assessing their success, explicitly reward those who did not take any more pieces than needed.

Another even more elusive task when dealing with excessive amounts of data is developing a sort of sixth sense or intuitive insight that allows you to recognize patterns in sets of data without necessarily having to break down or itemize each point. This skill is akin to discerning a shape from a discrete collection of points, and it is believed that the arts are particularly well suited to developing this sort of holistic approach to wading through data. Exposing students to data sets and encouraging them to try to figure out patterns of repetition of numbers, for example, could be a good primer.

Creativity

In almost every analysis of the 21st-century education challenge, writers, thinkers, and speakers all call out for the development of creativity as a paramount and defining skill, especially when referring to gaining a competitive advantage with regard to other nations and their educational systems.

Creativity and its sibling, the very fashionable innovation, are at the heart of technological advancement and may be the last bastion of self-esteem for the U.S. when compared with nations like China, Finland, Korea, Singapore, and others that dominate international education rankings.

The importance of creativity is undisputed within the 21st-century knowledge paradigm. The rationale is quite clear: in a world where context and not content is king, and where there is so much information available and remembering or accumulating knowledge has no value in itself, what really makes the difference is being able to think creatively and being able to translate ideas into the creation of things that have value.

However, despite this almost unanimous consensus about the importance of creativity, there is surprisingly scant literature or research about how students can learn creativity within the formal school setting. There are innumerable articles and opinion pieces that reaffirm the need to foster creativity in children, but there is no pedagogy of creativity that teachers can resort to in order to help cultivate the skill in their students.

Learning Creativity

Can you teach creativity? This question pops up quite naturally, and it would be difficult to dismiss it as irrelevant. But the answer is: "That it is the wrong question." There is a prejudice of sorts that a person is either born creative or not, and that it is more a personal characteristic or trait than a skill. The work of Carol Dweck (2007) and many other experts and cognitive researchers points to the fact that a growth mindset can overcome what seem to be innate characteristics and that, in effect, creativity, like intelligence, can be acquired through hard work and deliberate practice.

In analyzing 21st-century skills, the question of whether a particular skill can be taught or not is irrelevant, because the real question is whether that skill can be *learned*. In the particular case of creativity, the answer to the pertinent question is a resounding "yes." Creating the right conditions and fostering the development of the skill results in students becoming more creative.

As with any higher-order skill, the development of creative capacity requires deliberate techniques as well as a system of rewards that foster the successful application of the skill. Although there is a lack of research about how to teach creativity in school, outside of education there is a substantial body of research about how to catalyze the development of creativity as a skill. Research points to some systematic strategies that can help to ingrain creative attitudes in students:

- Systematically asking numerous questions.
- Challenging assumptions.
- Looking at the issues at hand from multiple points of view and perspectives.
- Allowing for the taking of risks.
- Creating an environment where mistakes are considered to be an important and necessary part of the learning process.
- Instilling confidence in students so that they feel that they have what it takes to come up with new ideas; fostering in students a sense of self-worth and confidence so that they are not inhibited about volunteering new approaches.
- Providing specific stimuli that prepare the mind for coming up with new and unique answers.

• Supplying encouragement in the face of creative blocks
as well as guiding students to pathways to break down
thinking so that the problem can be methodically ex-
plored from a different perspective in order to come up
with new ideas.

Most of these suggestions to encourage the learning of creativity
are rooted in common sense, and it does not seem impossible for a
classroom teacher to create conditions that foster the acquisition of
the skill, especially if the assessment system in place rewards creativity
explicitly.

Evaluating Creativity

All educators know the dirty little secret associated with anything we
do in class. Despite our best intentions, and even acknowledging that
intrinsic motivation should be the ultimate goal of schooling, in our
current school atmosphere, what does not get evaluated is not learned.
So, in order to realistically pursue our quest of learning creativity at
school, the skill must be assessed and rewarded within the regular class
context.

Assessing creativity may ultimately prove to be quite an elusive
proposition. Since creativity is considered a "soft" skill, defining objective parameters to gauge its development is inevitably going to be
somewhat counterintuitive, especially if we attempt not to use the
word "creative" in the rubric.

Searching on the Internet for "creativity rubric" will yield a number of results that reflect ongoing attempts to assess creativity and define criteria for degrees of creativity. Most of these rubrics include
some of the following parameters for evaluating creativity:

• Originality of the ideas expressed. The term "originality" may be somewhat subjective, but the concept can
be understood by students. The problem is that in order

for students to be original there must be a guiding process that allows them to learn how to tackle problems from multiple points of view so as to come up with original answers. Otherwise, we would resort back to the "fixed creativity" mindset that is antithetical to the development of that skill.

• Number of plausible ideas or alternative solutions that are formulated. This one is easier, since the rubric would attempt to encourage students to produce as many feasible answers as possible, forcing a nonjudgmental mindset, an inverse process from the traditionally bred instincts to converge toward the "best" answer, discarding the seemingly not so attractive alternatives for the sake of efficiency.

• Other derived criteria may include whether the answers presented are originated from more than one source, whether they are simple or complex, and whether they reuse or combine previous ideas or answers.

An important distinction needs to be made between assessing and evaluating, which, indeed, should be an objective in terms of the development of creativity in school, and measuring and grading. In her very interesting article "Assessing Creativity," Susan Brookhart (2013) takes a clear stance regarding whether creativity should be measured and/or graded. When referring to a creativity rubric included in the article, she candidly shares her point of view regarding the issue:

> I created this rubric with some trepidation—because where there's a rubric, there will be someone who's thinking of using it to grade. Generating a grade is not the intended purpose of the rubric for creativity. Rubrics help clarify criteria for success and show what the continuum of performance looks like, from low to high, from imitative to very creative. For that reason, rubrics are useful for sharing with students what they are

aiming for, where they are now, and what they should do next.
I do not recommend grading creativity.

There is a subtle difference, however, between grading creativity and rewarding creativity. Whereas grading implies creating different levels that would, eventually, match up with a grade, rewarding creativity may consist of adding bonus points for some of the desired embodiments of the skill.

Some possible examples of how to add the creativity dimension to our assignments and assessments include:

- Always include one or more open-ended questions— questions that do not have a single right answer but rather lend themselves to suggesting more than one answer. This can happen even in some of the less subjective disciplines, such as math and science.

- Include within the assessment rubric some bonus or extra points for creativity—not just for the quality of the answers offered but also for the number of feasible answers that students volunteer when answering open-ended questions.

- Convert physical spaces so that they foster creativity. In terms of the spaces themselves, there are many possible ways of making "creativity corners" or spots within the learning environment that are conducive to the development of the skill. Such examples include walls with markers where students can write or draw their ideas, and kinesthetic games that allow for the creation of models.

- Model creativity techniques in the context of classroom activities, often utilizing new and different media so as to take students away from their conventionally framed modes of thinking. It is important in this context to create a safe environment for the forwarding and presentation of ideas that is not judgmental, so as to avoid inhibiting creative efforts on the part of the students, who may fear that their ideas could be ridiculed or dismissed. It is important to convey to students that ideas that may seem outrageous at first glance can very well end up being more sensible and related to solutions than initially thought. Some creativity techniques include:

- Storm of ideas. When faced with a question, have students volunteer rapid-fire answers without any further comments being allowed; the facilitator records these ideas without any analysis or evaluation in this initial stage.

- Express ideas through images. Pose a textual question, then have students cut out images from a variety of sources such as magazines and brochures, and create a collage expressing in a nonlinear form what their proposed solutions to the problem may be. Another creative means of expression could be music. There are some fascinating experiments where groups use simple instruments to try to express musically the answer to a question. For instance, students may be called out to compose a short piece using very straightforward instruments that require no musical training to describe a physical or chemical phenomenon.

Introducing creativity into the curriculum is, in itself, quite a creative endeavor, so there is no single right answer. The process to account for the learning of this skill within the school curriculum can be approached using the same tools and mindset that have been described to help students learn it. Introducing creativity in schools requires creativity, so at heart, it's really a matter of cultivating creativity in adult educators.

Critical Thinking

Another star in the 21st-century skills movement is critical thinking. In order to survive in the data-rich, intrinsically dynamic, and fast-paced environment of the 21st century, there are more onerous requirements than in the pre-Internet era, when information was more stable, there were fewer choices, and the pace of change was manageable. Aspiring lifelong learners have to expand the variety and number of tools in their toolboxes if they want to deal with the uncertainty and unpredictability of the wonderful new knowledge era.

Critical thinking allows us to be able to hold our own intellectually—to process complexity and change while remaining anchored within a sense of self and strengthening our fundamental beliefs and values.

Defining critical thinking is a difficult challenge. At The Critical Thinking Community, the starting definition is taken from a statement presented at the Eighth Annual International Conference on Critical Thinking and Education Reform, way back in 1987:

> Critical thinking is the intellectually disciplined process of actively and skillfully conceptualizing, applying, analyzing, synthesizing, and/or evaluating information gathered from, or generated by, observation, experience, reflection, reasoning, or communication, as a guide to belief and action. In its exemplary form, it is based on universal intellectual values that transcend subject matter divisions: clarity, accuracy, precision, consistency, relevance, sound evidence, good reasons, depth, breadth, and fairness.

Even though this scholarly definition is admirable, it challenges us to do a little bit of critical thinking ourselves, because despite its elegance it does little to clarify what it entails to produce good critical thinkers in the classroom. When referring to 21st-century skills, it is quite unnecessary to come up with a precise definition. The concept of critical thinking is understandable; we do not need to dissect it to be able to generate a school curriculum that addresses the learning of the skill. This is an extremely important principle in 21st-century education, and, at the risk of being repetitive, I tend to stress it over and over again. Unlike the pre-Internet environment, when we did attempt to narrowly define and precisely determine outcomes for learning, processes that involve the development of 21st-century skills are going to be rather messy and chaotic by nature, and the journey itself is more important than the destination.

Any attempts by educators to introduce elements into the curriculum that specifically address the learning of critical thinking as a skill are bound to elicit different responses in students, some of which are not entirely measurable. The good news is that there is an ample body of literature that covers how to break down critical thinking into other more manageable skills, as well as a treasure trove of resources and lesson plans on how to develop the skill in the classroom setting.

The bad news is that there is no simple sequence of steps that will produce standard results in all students and that could guarantee that they will develop into critical thinkers. However, just focusing on the issue, even with an approach that perforce is going to be imperfect, will make a huge impact on the development of the skill in students.

Teachers, when planning their units, should design their classroom activities so that they foster critical thinking, and also should recognize the need to develop the skill and make it a major objective within their mission in the classroom. It is not enough to pay lip service to the development of these higher-order 21st-century skills. Even if we cannot come up with a standardized test that measures the development and progress of critical thinking and other such skills in our students, holding students accountable for their critical thinking and giving them qualitative feedback on their progress makes a substantial positive difference.

In the normal classroom situation, teachers are looking for the mastery of certain concepts and content, and the rigorous do-or-die judgment is proffered exclusively based on whether students are able to demonstrate that they have acquired proficiency in those areas. In an environment where the importance of critical thinking and other 21st-century skills is recognized, teachers will create rubrics that also account for whether students are acquiring these higher-order skills.

A Pedagogy for Critical Thinking

There is a lot of information on the Internet about the technical nuances of learning critical thinking. But regardless of the specific implementation, there are some general principles that can help us determine the main drivers for a critical thinking–oriented pedagogy:

- **Minimize lecturing.** Moving away from spoon-feeding content to our students is a trait of the 21st-century pedagogy that is not exclusive to critical thinking. But in this case it is right on the mark, because in order to develop independent thinking and encourage students to process information on their own, it is necessary that, within the limits allowed by the students' level of understanding of the topic at hand, the teacher step away as much as possible from pre-digesting knowledge and allow students to, literally, think as much as possible.

- **Use questioning.** Questioning is a venerable classroom activity that has long been acknowledged as eliciting thinking skills in students. Looking at a problem or issue and framing relevant questions about it has long been acknowledged as one of the most important thinking skills, since it forces students to actively analyze content in a way that activates thinking.

- **Assign Writing.** Writing is beneficial in all its forms, but nonfiction writing and reflective writing have always been on the short list of inquiry-based activities that foster a formal embodiment of the thinking process in a way that can then be shared with others, thus materializing the thinking process.

- **Embody critical thinking.** As with most 21st-century skills, we want to create a self-fulfilling prophecy of sorts in our classroom interactions. The adult facilitating the learning process should make frequent and explicit references to the thinking process, and should lead collective classroom thinking exercises when analyzing a topic. Modeling the skill itself will pass on an important message to students as to what is expected of them in the classroom context.

- **Break down critical thinking into manageable strategies.** Most of the learning strategies associated with critical thinking available on the Internet tend to break down the critical thinking process into a series of other mental skills (such as analysis, deduction, inference, etc.) that can be discretely accounted for and analyzed in the critical thinking process. It is important to debunk the idea that critical thinking, or any other higher-order thinking skill, is exclusively intuitive and innate, and therefore impossible to learn systematically. When the teacher takes a moment to address how to break down critical thinking into a subset of thinking skills, it clarifies the strategies that students can learn to apply to their own critical thinking process, but it also makes a strong statement to the effect that the skill can, indeed, be learned.

- **Extending the scientific method.** The scientific method has been the backbone of the spinoff skills learned in science. Through a systematic and scientific approach to problem solving, science defines an inquiry-based process to analyze variables, data, and observations, and to formulate hypotheses and conclusions from all that is learned in the process. Extending the scope of the scientific method approach beyond science can be a healthy way to develop critical thinking skills. Even though the scientific method cannot be applied to everything, it is a good starting point to exemplify how the solving of a problem can be broken down into a series of steps, and how arriving at a conclusion can be a methodical process that is based on objective data and observations. Needless to say, science can be one of the best subjects in which to develop critical thinking skills, so curriculum decisions must be made in order to allow for enough time in the schedule to address the inquiry-based scientific process.

Creating a pedagogy that fosters critical thinking is not an exact science, and teachers should not be intimidated by the many sources that each claim to have the exclusive proprietary approach to developing critical thinking skills. Undoubtedly, reflecting about our own critical thinking processes will always serve us well in trying to develop this habit in our students. Developing a 21st-century pedagogy and addressing the learning of 21st-century skills is a 21st-century exercise for educators also, and calls into question many of our professional development methods and the way we approach our own practice. We need to work hard at becoming more reflective practitioners as a first necessary and decisive step toward creating the 21st-century school.

Imagination

I firmly believe that the new knowledge paradigm offers unprecedented opportunities for learning, and that when we finally are able to tap into the unlimited potential of this new learning scenario we shall be able to substantially improve our quality of living. There are, however, some drawbacks, and the transition between the fixed-knowledge scenario and the current one of infinite abundance is bound to result in some holes.

We are fond of saying to the young ones that in our time, we were able to have lots of fun by simply conjuring worlds of imagination: using a broomstick or any other prop, we could imagine and dream up adventures, and today's children are missing out on those wonderful worlds of fantasy that we created. The truth is, deep down, most adults would love to be children in this era, with immersive, realistic video game environments that bring an unprecedented level of interaction and realism to play.

But there is an element of truth in reminiscing about the good old days that has an implication in terms of the learning experience. Because we had to dream up makeshift scenarios for our fun, children in the pre-Internet generation had to exercise their imaginations in ways that now are viewed as completely unnecessary. Children today seldom need to use their imaginations at all, since almost anything can be found on the Internet or in a game environment.

If we accept that creativity is a necessary skill for the 21st century, we should be concerned about this diminished imaginative capacity, since imagination is a precursor for creativity. Bottom line, our children need to learn how to imagine more in order to develop the mental skills that will serve them well in the 21st century.

Should we teach imagination in school? Is it possible to teach imagination within the context of the formal school system? Again, it is not about whether we can teach it; it is about whether students can learn it. Manufacturers of new technological devices that stretch visualization capabilities and developers of the latest games that leave no room for imagination will not come up with an educational program that will counteract the effects of transporting children almost physically to these realms without having any need to develop projective thinking skills. Instead of asking whether we should do it, we need to do what is right and not play any blame game, even if it is deemed unfair that these firms are making all the profits and we are left to deal with their intended or unintended but quite profound impact on children.

Learning to Imagine

Skills don't get much murkier than imagination, especially when it comes to finding a way to include the formal learning of this skill in the curriculum. Our teaching reflexes are not attuned to teaching and subsequently assessing imagination.

However, again, common sense comes to our rescue, and although there aren't any ready-made lesson plans on the Internet designed to facilitate learning imagination, there are certain activities that are bound to stimulate students' ability to imagine:

- **Visualization exercises.** Visualization involves teams coming up with images of some future events or developments. The most common way of doing this is to have students close their eyes as a narrator guides them through scenarios and asks them to attempt to visualize what is going on. A possible related development includes later writing about and reflecting on whatever has been visualized. The objective is to train the students to isolate themselves from external stimuli in order to create visual scenarios in their mind's eye. Doing so provides them with a rare opportunity to engage in a mental process starting with a clean slate, which, given today's multiplicity of sometimes confusing stimuli, can be a welcome break from everyday reality. Visualizations are a common strategy to stimulate creativity amongst adults, and are frequently used in the creation of strategic plans and at executive retreats to help participants think outside the box. There are multiple opportunities to use visualization as a regular part of the academic work being done in school.

- **"Bare-bones" exercises.** A more extreme but nonetheless interesting strategy for learning imagination in the school context consists of deliberately planned "survival" simulations, where students have to use basic elements, such as just pen and paper, or whatever props are appropriate for the activity, to solve a problem or create something without accessing the Internet, textbooks, or computers. One example of such an activity is the "black box" experiment, where students are given a cardboard box with things inside that they cannot see. The objective of the experiment is to try to find out what is inside by moving, shaking, and doing whatever is possible to the box without compromising its structural integrity. At the same time, students have to estimate basic measurements such as length, width, height, and weight in order to better define the box and to try to guess what the contents are. The work is generally done in small groups, which can share what their conclusions are. In a dramatic final touch, the teacher collects the boxes from students, who, by that time, are absolutely desperate to open them up and see what the correct answer might be. The answer, the teacher then says, is not what people would see if they opened the box, but what they themselves have decided must be inside it, through their best reasoning. A parallel can be drawn to the scientists who imagined the structure of the atom: at the end of the day, they could not open up the atom and see what was inside, but only work with a model that they created based on their knowledge, and refine it successively.

- **Engaging students through hypothetical scenarios.** Whenever possible, teachers can introduce within class discussions hypothetical project scenarios and "what if" questions that actively engage students in coming up

with possible developments and analyzing their consequences. For example, ask students to write a paper on
what would have happened if Hitler had not committed
suicide, or if Japan had not capitulated after the bombing of Hiroshima and Nagasaki.

Trying to evaluate and assess imagination may stretch the concept
of 21st-century skills a little too far. Regular assessment activities that
involve the use of imagination would definitely suffice, without the
need to come up with a rubric that explicitly incorporates imagination
as a desired trait.

Collaboration

The most flagrant disconnect between school and the real world is the
lack of collaboration. Whether students end up working in a sophisticated high-tech environment or spend their days engaged in manual
labor, it is unlikely that they will be working in isolation.

From the moment that students step outside the world of formal
schooling, they start working on teams, further aided by the endless
possibilities that technology offers for effective collaboration across
distances. In every professional realm—and this comes up repeatedly
when recruiters are asked what the most desirable traits are in a job
candidate—workers are called upon to perform as functional and effective contributors to teams. But schools still operate under a rigorously created environment in which all work is individual and, more
importantly, accountability is also individual. Instead of being the
norm and the predominant modality for schoolwork, collaboration
is the exception.

The dreaded "group project" has been in place forever in classrooms, but now it is one of the most relevant 21st-century skills, and
it is the development of this skill that can benefit the most from the
successful introduction of technology for learning.

There is no need to review strategies for introducing collaboration in the classroom, since every educator has made a stab at this. The real imperative is to make collaboration a more frequent and relevant mode of work, in such a way that it is almost intrinsic to the learning experience. Of particular importance is how collaborative work is planned, how the teams are formed, what the expectations are for each of the members and for the team itself, and how the work is assessed.

Planning. Considering our modern-day realization that learning is not one dimensional and that it is the job of the school to help all children rise up to their full potential, collaborative work constitutes a unique opportunity to develop assignments where each member of the team can contribute in a different way. Planning activities such that there are components that cater to different learning styles will not only add to the value of the product itself, but also add to the sense of worth and self-esteem of all members of the team, who thus feel that they can contribute to the success of the group. When designing these activities, it is important to take into account that there should be different skills that need to be demonstrated as desired outcomes of the project, so that the work involved is not merely the sum of similarly targeted efforts on the part of team members.

How the teams are formed. If the work is designed taking into account multiple skill sets, it is essential that teachers do not leave it up to students to form their own teams based on friendship or other preferences. A properly designed collaborative project that requires diverse contributions from the team members will require the teacher to select members of the team based on how they can individually contribute to the team. For example, if the project entails some kind of visual presentation, there should be one member of the team who is especially good at either designing presentations or visual communication. If formal research is part of the activity, every team should have one member who is of the "academic type." In both cases, it is important to make sure that other skills are also required to complete the project.

Expectations for each of the members of the team. Within this scenario in which the members of the team can all contribute to the extent of their styles and abilities, it is important that expectations are very clearly spelled out in terms of roles. For example, the visual media master cannot be the one who just puts together the information in a way that is visually appealing without having any idea what the content of the work is. It needs to be clarified that the team should analyze the different roles and functions to be fulfilled in successfully completing the assignment, and that each team member should have primary responsibility for one of those areas and secondary responsibility for monitoring, overseeing, and collaborating with the people responsible for each other area as well.

Assessment of collaborative work. Until that golden time when intrinsic motivation reigns supreme, and students are no longer asking about what will be on the test, but rather what is relevant for their learning, assessment will still drive effort, so the evaluation of collaborative work should include not just a measure of accountability for individual contributions, but also, and even more importantly, a measure of how the participation of all members of the team provides greater value for the result of the project itself. For example, a reflection that should be present in any rubric that gauges collaborative work is: In what ways is this project better because it has been carried out by a team and not by individuals? This compels students to reflect on the work they have done, and sends a clear message that the whole is expected to be greater than the sum of its parts.

I have refrained from discussing how collaboration can take place, because the actual mode in which students effectively collaborate is not important in itself, and not being prescriptive about the method conveys implicitly that collaboration should be as spontaneous and natural as possible. It is also unnecessary to tell students how they can work together; classroom experience shows that they will find a way easily enough. Many of us have been stopped in our tracks when we aggressively reprimanded students for being on Facebook during class, when they show us with outraged innocence that the only reason they are on the social network is that their teammate is using that medium to send out information or link to a resource needed for work.

Teachers are not known for being very open to collaboration with peers. One good way to foster a collaborative environment in the classroom is to make good on the promise of professional learning communities and to find ways to reach out to our colleagues, so that planning and reflection on our own practice become as ubiquitous and as natural as student collaboration.

Globalization

It goes without saying that the world is irreversibly globalized and interconnected. Advances in telecommunication have resulted in a world in which we are able to see what is happening on the other side of the globe in real time, and to interact with increasing levels of realism with people throughout the world.

The possibilities that globalization opens up regarding education are endless. Having the whole world a few keystrokes away is a dream come true for any teacher, as it means we can extend the learning experience in unlimited ways beyond the confines of the classroom. But it also presents us with a formidable challenge. There is a dire need to prepare our students to interact with the global interconnected world, so that the ensuing stimuli can be processed in ways that are positive, that are not seen as threatening or disruptive, and that do not conspire against building a strong sense of identity.

The accepted mantra for globalization is "think global, act local," and that is, indeed, a good overarching guide for how to approach the issue of globalization.

How do we help our students acquire a global mindset? By embodying, in our classroom interactions, a global mindset by virtue of the resources used for learning, the nature of classroom activities, and even the way we, the adults, conduct ourselves in that context. A global classroom will foster a global mindset.

Just as students don't think of technology as "technology—a special category of things to be learned," since they have grown up surrounded by technology and innovations and they form part of kids' habitual landscape, a truly global mindset does not consider globalization as a specialty or an activity to be consciously engaged in. Coming up with projects that include a globalized dimension should be absolutely natural for teachers and students at this point.

The most commonly brandished reason for learning about globalization is related to the outsourcing phenomenon, and how in the global economy, if Americans do not become globally competitive, people from China, India, and other countries will steal their jobs. This competitive motive does not sit well with the younger generation and is not an intrinsically motivating factor. That rhetoric may have worked in the 1960s, but now, when in general the younger generations are, thankfully, acting out of deeper meaning and motivation, it is not enough to constitute an ethical imperative. The real reason that globalization should be at the forefront of many activities in the school setting is because the open and level playing field provides us with unprecedented opportunities to learn from each other, to know about other cultures, and to truly embrace the spirit of global brotherhood. Espousing the values of tolerance and multiculturalism is an objective in itself, and a defining trait of citizenship in the 21st century.

Learning Globalization

There is no standard defined set of steps that unequivocally help students learn globalization. The basic principle is to assign projects that include an international dimension and that allow students to learn about elements of other cultures and, whenever possible, to engage in live interactions with their peers across the world. Some strategies and related activities include:

- **Collaborative projects with students from schools in a different physical location.** A logical primary recommendation for learning about globalization is engaging in collaborative projects with students from schools in different places in the world. There are many Web sites that act as repositories for such projects and that also feature pages where teachers who are interested in looking for partners for collaborative endeavors advertise, often including categorization of projects by subject matter, objectives, and age level. Some of the desirable characteristics of these projects would be:

  - Assignments that target content and skills that are common to all the schools participating in the project. This entails teachers exchanging extensive information regarding the work they do in class, so as to ensure that the project is meaningful for all involved.

  - Groups made up of team members from different schools. Teams will be integrated, with each team including students from each school participating in the project, if possible in equal proportions, so that students have to interact with each other to complete the assignment.

  - Common assessment criteria. The assessment rubric and the grade obtained by the members of the team should be common, and valid for each of the schools participating. This ensures that assessment is consistent and that all students are equally motivated to perform well.

  - Freedom to find the best medium for collaboration. As we have said before, it is not necessary to tell students how they have to get in touch to produce the work. Students can achieve this without any intervention, and in a natural and spontaneous way.

- Assignments with a local flavor. It would be a good idea to include some local cultural element as part of the project, so that students can showcase their roots, and also learn about other cultures.

- Assessment criteria that take into account the globalization factor. Students should be assessed not only on how successfully they complete the project and whether they meet the academic standards and objectives, but also the degree and extent to which their interaction with their teammates from across the globe has resulted in positive results, how much they learned about their teammates' culture, and how well local cultural factors were highlighted, etc.

- Joint presentation of the project by all students on the team. If possible, it would be ideal to set up a final session where students in the different schools are connected via Skype or some other similar service, and share a joint oral presentation of the project, thus adding to the level of interaction and effectively breaking down the distance between the team members and creating a global classroom. Even if the academic results are not outstanding, the emotional and ethical growth that such an experience fosters can be unparalleled. The objective of these globalized projects is to open up the four walls of the classroom in ways that model the globalization mindset for students.

- **Globalized sources for learning.** A great way to cultivate a global mindset is for the adults facilitating the learning process to make frequent reference to how the particular topic or issue being discussed is dealt with at different locales all over the world. Consistently looking for international sources for the topics studied and making reference to current events will do the trick. And doing this helps broaden perspectives and increase understanding about the issue being studied. The teacher who wants to create a globalized environment in the classroom will bring the world into the classroom, and there are limitless opportunities to do so.

Educators must embrace a global mindset themselves in order to transmit this value to their students. It would be hard to convey to students the need to broaden their horizons and truly be open to ideas from different places in the world if we as professional practitioners are not trying to learn from other countries and their educational systems.

Future 21st-Century Skills

As we have stressed over and over again, this is not a complete list; as the knowledge model evolves and changes, other skills are bound to appear that need to be addressed in school. But the principles of 21st-century learning, upon which these skills are based, are not going to go away. There might be new technological innovations, but lifelong learning is going to remain the ultimate goal of the educational system.

All it takes for teachers to keep abreast of these changes is to have a learning mindset—to want to keep on learning, read as much as possible, look for multiple sources, and basically take advantage of the new and unprecedented opportunities that will continue to open up for continuous learning. Sounds like a piece of cake, right? Well, no, of course not. However, it is worth the effort. The foundation upon which the skills mentioned here are based will also apply to the acquisition of future skills, and attempting to help our students learn these skills will make a big difference in their lives.

CHAPTER EIGHT

Neuroscience

So far, we have described extensively some of the changes in the underlying knowledge paradigm and how they impact education. These changes were brought about by the development of the Internet and the ensuing access to nearly infinite information. The challenge ahead of us is formidable, since we need to define a whole new pedagogy to confront this abruptly changed scenario. But all of those changes stem from a change in the conditions for education, and are not new discoveries.

Teachers have, throughout history, relied on their own perceptions and analysis of reality in order to define strategies to improve their teaching in a way that impacted the learning of their students. Although a gigantic volume of educational theory was developed over the years, even withholding judgment on the effectiveness of such analyses and speculations and the real impact they may have in the classroom, whatever advances have been made in teaching and learning have all come out of our observations, research on the effects of strategies, and conclusions drawn from the application of the strategies and techniques. Over the many centuries during which education was refined, practically no major discoveries were made about learning.

All that is on the verge of changing. The still nascent discipline of neuroscience, the study of the brain, and, in particular, its applications to education, promises discoveries that will lead to new ideas and strategies and will support a new pedagogy that is based on scientific discoveries about how the brain works and what mechanisms need to be activated for learning. With the aid of new imaging technology that can map the brain in real time as thought processes are taking place, scientists are rapidly gaining ground in understanding the brain as never before, which can be evidenced by the increased activity in research institutions, conferences, papers, and books that report periodically on the results of brain-related research.

As an example, one of the myths regarding the brain that has been dispelled by the findings in neuroscience is that a very small percentage of the brain is actually used; newer research shows that most of the areas of the brain are utilized in one form or other. It will be interesting to see what use that new information will eventually be put to.

When it comes to education, the promise is clear: neuroscience will deliver better understanding of how the brain works, cognitive functions, how learning occurs, different learning styles and profiles, the regions that are activated for certain mental processes, and how the brains of people with learning difficulties function. This will result in specific ideas and strategies that will help trigger a more efficient learning process, and more importantly, one that targets every individual in the right way so as to help all students reach their full potential.

Coupling neuroscience with technology and combining this new-found information about the brain with the latest innovations could result in breakthrough software that, for example, could provide an adaptive learning experience that customizes learning based on the software's detection of learning ability and style, to produce a unique interactive learning experience.

Brain-Based Education

Although a great deal of progress has been made in neuroscience, as can be attested by the almost daily reports of new findings regarding the understanding of the brain, there is a gap between research and implementation—there are not a lot of applications of that research to the hard reality of the classroom. And educators seem to be harboring this sort of guilty feeling that they are not up-to-date on the latest findings and, as such, they're missing out on some truly revolutionary applications of neuroscience.

To make matters more confusing, in this era in which self-proclaimed expertise is almost the norm, a number of products' creators claim their products are based on neuroscience data and have been "proved" to work. More often than not these programs are extensive—involving long periods of learning and training—as well as expensive, and therefore are not a feasible option for budget-deprived schools.

The phrase "brain-based education" loosely refers to the application of neuroscience concepts and findings to the classroom environment. The million-dollar question is, what is available now that really makes sense in terms of transforming the learning experience? And here is where, despite all the advances, a word of caution is needed. Despite the enormous potential of the application of neuroscience in the classroom, as of yet there aren't any products that can directly make a significant impact without a relevant contribution and adaptation on the part of the teacher. As for the claims of proven results based on research, Judy Willis, a very well-known researcher, teacher, and advocate for the application of neuroscience in education, very clearly dispels such claims: "My basic recommendation is that if a product claims to be proven by brain research, forget it. Nothing from the lab can be proven to work in the classroom—it can only correlate" (Bernard, 2010).

Neuroscience research continues to advance, and will eventually result in tools that will bridge the gap between research and implementation. In the meantime, educators should endeavor to understand the principles that are guiding the neuroscience research, and how those principles can be translated into improved classroom practice.

Neuroplasticity

In order to understand the scope of possible applications of the findings of neuroscience in the classroom, we need to start with the origin of the research. The concept that undergirds most of the findings in neuroscience is that of neuroplasticity, which basically has to do with the ability of the brain to rewire itself in such a way that areas of the brain that normally perform one function can change to learn new functions. It was once widely believed that neuroplasticity was almost exclusive to early childhood, but what scientists are finding is that neuroplasticity still continues as people grow older, and they are working on methods that can stimulate the process.

As more is discovered about the way the brain functions and which areas are associated with different tasks and mental processes, hopefully scientists will be able to find out which processes, specifically associated with learning strategies, can trigger the development of the brain to achieve the desired effects. A hypothetical "holy grail" of neuroscience as it applies to learning would be a correlation between causes and effects—a list of learning strategies that would trigger a rewiring of the brain so that it is able to perform the desired function.

Unfortunately, scientists are still far from being able to draw up such a list. However, though they are not yet fully formed, some of the ideas in neuroscience have very important implications regarding pedagogical applications.

Intelligence and other mental capabilities are not fixed in supply. One of the most important implications of neuroplasticity is that it confirms what good teachers have always known: that there is no limit to what people can achieve given the right motivation and enough practice. Labeling students as unintelligent, noncreative, or not capable of developing certain mental skills becomes a negative self-fulfilling prophecy. In her groundbreaking book *Mindset: The New Psychology of Success* (2007), Carol Dweck makes a very solid case for positive psychology based on research findings and also on what neuroscience has discovered about the brain being able to rewire itself. In terms of classroom application, it should be clear by now that students' capabilities have no limit, and they should be stimulated to the fullest extent possible. This "growth mindset," as Dweck has labeled it, has been proved by research to produce positive results. If there is one capital sin that teachers should avoid at all costs in the 21st century, it is underestimating students' capacities in a way that sets them up for failure.

Different learning styles. It is undeniable that the more we know about how the brain works, the more we must accept that not all learners learn the same way. At this point, it is impossible to predict which students will be suited to which learning styles, but teachers should be aware that the differences in the way our brains have been wired make it so that each of us finds it easier to learn in certain ways. The consequences are obvious but not always followed up on. If we consistently teach and assess in the same way, we are not doing all students a disservice by reducing the learning experience to a one-dimensional process, but we are doing some students an even greater disservice, by causing them to fall behind if the teaching and assessing style we have chosen is not the style that best suits their brains.

We need to focus on the strengths, but not forget the weaknesses. Scientific data about neuroplasticity tells us that the brain can be extensively retrained, so even though we want to focus on developing strengths, a healthy balanced diet of mental activity also requires that we target those areas that are not so well developed, especially in the formative years, so that students can improve those capabilities.

Reflecting on our own learning. When students are encouraged to reflect on their own learning, the metacognitive reflection process is beneficial to the learning itself, and it helps cultivate a growth mindset in students. Increasing students' awareness of their mental processes and how they need to play to their strengths and practice to improve their weaknesses helps them take ownership of their learning and adopt a growth mindset. It is also consistent with our ultimate quest for lifelong learning: being able to reflect on one's own learning and check it against learning targets is an indispensable skill, especially if students can perform it without the reassurance of an adult or teacher mentor. There are innumerable ways to do this, such as keeping journals. The important thing is that a strong belief in the fact that the brain can be developed and basic knowledge about how that happens can constitute a virtuous circle that fosters effective learning. As always, the adult learners (a.k.a. the teachers) should model this by reflecting on their own learning profiles, and should prominently portray themselves as learners.

It is clear that brain flexibility is both desirable and achievable, that multiple learning styles need to be catered to in school, that tips and hints about brain stimulation can be verified by empirical findings in the classroom, and that, of course, it is always a good idea to pay attention to the individual characteristics of our students.

The Tools and Strategies

Even though most of them are not ready to be immediately implemented in the classroom, there are a number of tools and strategies based in neuroscience that have been merged into programs and software available for possible use in the educational setting. It is interesting to explore them so as to make informed decisions about whether to adopt them or not.

Learning profiles. One of the initial mainstream applications of neuroscience research, which provides the foundation for most of the professional development courses that are available through private companies and higher education institutions, has to do with channeling what is known about the brain into mental models that can then be translated into learning profiles. These models can help educators understand how their students learn, help them interpret students' behaviors, and, in an ideal world, help them come up with strategies that are specifically directed to addressing whatever learning roadblocks are encountered so that students can progress. Learning about the way the brain works can, of course, be very useful, and can trigger a process of thinking about learning in a different way, as well as raising teachers' levels of awareness regarding brain-based education. However, for commercial reasons, these companies are trying to sell their mental models as if they were real-life dissections of the brain. Despite their refinement and complexity, these models are just theoretical constructs that attempt to categorize what is still a very complex issue; it is not as though, if we were to open up the skull, the brain would be neatly labeled. These mental models are not, and can never be, universal, so applying them indiscriminately as if they were the new gospel of learning is bound to meet with failure and frustration, as well as dangerously expecting students to perform to certain predetermined outcomes. Learning about these models is very useful, but I would recommend that more than one framework be studied so as to stress the fact that none of these theoretical models are, in themselves, infallible. An overall increased knowledge about the functioning of the brain could undoubtedly be beneficial for teachers, and, in some cases, some of the strategies prescribed may indeed work for students who match the conducts that were observed during the companies' research, which forms the basis for these courses.

Adaptive technologies. When technology meets neuroscience, we enter the realm of adaptive technologies. The concept is very simple and holds almost infinite potential. The idea is that the computer interacts with the user in a way that detects, to as great an extent as possible, the user's learning style, dominant abilities, and general learning potential. Delving into a preloaded database of activities and questions, the ensuing delivery of instruction to that user is tailored to the individual characteristics of the person using the program, and is updated and corrected in real time. The UK-based Royal Society

(Blakemore, 2011), a prestigious research group composed of notable individuals from all fields and disciplines, outlines the potential of adaptive technologies within its Brain Waves project:

> Digital technologies can be developed to support individualised self-paced learning and highly specialised practice in a game-like way. Interactive games of this kind use a teacher-pupil model to adapt the task to the learner's needs, and a task model to provide meaningful feedback on their actions. This means interactive technologies can provide personalized help on a daily basis in a way that is difficult to achieve in a demanding classroom environment.

There are an increasing number of adaptive technologies that are gradually finding their way into being feasible classroom activities. Teachers should be attentive and attuned to these novelties, since they really can make a big difference in terms of materializing the promise of 21st-century education. It will only be a matter of time until they become commonplace in the classroom.

Cognitive tutoring. Cognitive tutoring is one of the most promising applications of adaptive technologies. Based on cognitive psychology, the proposition is that a computer program interacts with the student and, initially, detects the student's learning profile and then tailors the delivery of exercises through problems, activities, and other instructional tasks based on that individualized profile. The leader in this area is a private company called Carnegie Learning, founded by researchers at Carnegie Mellon University. The company offers programs and software that apply cognitive tutoring to the learning of mathematics. There are also many other third-party applications that build upon cognitive psychology to deliver customized instructional technology. The jury is still out on cognitive tutoring, since there are somewhat conflicting reports regarding the effectiveness of such programs. However, whether using such programs improves test scores on traditional assessments isn't necessarily relevant, since the whole concept of measurement in education is in itself terribly controversial. Also, it can be argued that the process itself is valuable and should be "protected" from being evaluated merely based on standardized outcomes. This application of adaptive technologies does hold promise, and will undoubtedly yield better results in the future.

Brain Gym. One of the most controversial intended implementations of neuroscience is what is generically known, and commercially patented, as "Brain Gym." The claim is that, through specific exercises that stimulate sensory motor coordination, students will be able to learn better. As would be expected, the company selling Brain Gym programs cites a number of research cases and presents evidence for the positive effects and success of the program. There is, obviously, a certain logic to the whole proposition, since we all know from our own experience that the physical disposition of our bodies will, indeed, impact our ability to learn. However, it is hard to accept that a universal set of exercises will really predispose all learners in the same way. After a long and tedious session of passively listening, everyone in the audience would benefit from stretching and walking around, but moving from there to a standardized series of exercises that supposedly will trigger very intense learning is a long stretch. Brain Gym is one of the most often ridiculed applications of neuroscience; any search of the term on the Internet will bring up some pretty strongly worded pieces blasting Brain Gym as pseudoscience. A particularly funny such attack was published in the "Bad Science" column in *The Guardian* (Goldacre, 2008) and is hilariously titled "Banging Your Head Repeatedly Against the Brick Wall of Teachers' Stupidity Helps Increase Blood Flow to Your Frontal Lobes." This controversy can shed light on the fact that the applications of neuroscience are still young enough to elicit this sort of conflict, and to place teachers at a crossroads in terms of the implicit pressure received from reading so much about these possible applications and a certain intuition that it could be more hype than substance.

Brain exercises. Brain exercises seek to apply neuroscience findings to computer activities that stimulate the development of mental skills. Headed by Lumosity, a commercial company whose applications are used by millions of people worldwide, these brain exercises seek to stimulate the development of certain mental capacities and to, in the case of older adults, maintain those capabilities as we grow older. It is hard to find hard evidence either for or against the use of such programs, but it seems to be a positive proposition and, eventually, we can expect to be able to substantiate the effectiveness of these exercises with some more verifiable data. Can they be used in the classroom? Certainly prescribing brain exercises to students to attempt to improve their memory or other cognitive functions will not hurt them. The question is: is it more worthwhile to do brain exercises that target the development of math skills in a 21st-century computerized way or to learn those skills through traditional arithmetic drills?

Programs for learning disorders. One of the main problems with developing real-life classroom applications of neuroscience findings is the difficulty of generalizing strategies. As we narrow down our focus to certain specific issues that require intervention, neurodevelopmental research can become more helpful. There are a number of products that claim to address issues associated with learning difficulties, in particular those associated with reading. Of those, perhaps the most noteworthy one is Fast ForWord, reading intervention software built upon the pioneering work of Dr. Paula Tallal and her team of researchers. Again, the data related to the effectiveness of this and other similar programs is inconclusive, but there seems to be a valid scientific basis at play. The program is based on how the detection of different tones at an early age can impact reading comprehension and modifies the way texts are read in order to improve the chances of recognition by students. The way the text is modified is based on a diagnostic procedure that takes into account the ability of the subject in question to detect the difference between two tones that are played adjacently. FastForWord is, by far, the most widely implemented neuroscience application in schools and the first one to become a well-known mainstream program that is based on neuroscience. It is still too early to make a final judgment on the effectiveness of the program, since it will take years of substantive research to provide enough data. It will be interesting to follow whether the program ultimately ends up being successful. All in all, helping students with learning disabilities is an area that may profit greatly from neuroscience applications, and it is a good idea to watch out for further developments.

The Future of Neuroscience

The application of neuroscience to the classroom holds immense promise but, as of yet, opportunities for implementation are few and their effectiveness is largely unproved, due to the fact that neuroscience research is a young field, and also that research on the efficacy of a particular program takes years.

However, as imaging techniques continue to improve and more is learned about the inner workings of the brain we can expect that an increasing number of products and tested strategies will become available. In particular, adaptive technologies that produce an interactive, engaging, and customized experience for every student could very well become a major protagonist in the future of education. For the time being, it is important for educators to keep an eye open to new developments and findings.

CHAPTER NINE

Multimedia

The invention of the printing press was a turning point in terms of how education and culture, until then restricted to the possessors of valuable manuscripts, could be extended to the masses. The development of the Internet was a similar breakthrough in extending the reach of knowledge. In both cases, the preferred medium was the written word. Both almost exclusively relied on the written word to relay that cultural expansion, and the initial years of the Internet saw an exponential growth of mostly text-based pages. If anything, the overwhelming amount of text available just a few keystrokes away stressed the need to develop finely honed skills related to reading comprehension and writing. School curricula remained relevant, given that, ever since the printed book became the dominant form of transmitting information, increased emphasis was rightly placed on helping students develop advanced skills for decoding and producing text, the almost exclusive form for learning and sharing that learning.

And then, almost serendipitously, like most innovations that happen on the Internet, something changed dramatically. Computers featured unbelievably more powerful processors, graphics cards were able to conjure stunning displays, hard disk storage became increasingly inexpensive, digital cameras that could also shoot video took over the photography market, every portable device included a camera of sorts, and video editing software started being not only more affordable but also easier to use. Coupled with these technological advances, free video hosting services such as YouTube opened up an unprecedented and limitless world of multimedia access for everybody.

In the space of just a few years, computer users went from having access to a handful of CD-based videos to being able to find just about any video clip they wanted on YouTube or another hosting service. Ever since, the written word has seen its preeminence slowly but decisively being challenged by a younger form of expression: videos.

Almost in parallel with this transformation, Microsoft created one of the most maligned and yet most-used pieces of software in history: PowerPoint. The massive use of PowerPoint in workplace presentations to combine images with text changed the landscape of professional presentations completely, moving away from the previously unchallenged lengthy written report to oral presentations that combine images, video, sometimes audio, and text.

Regardless of value judgments, which would be pointless, about whether the growth and dominance of multimedia is intrinsically good or bad, the inescapable truth is that as increasing amounts of multimedia are consumed, most functioning adults will be called upon to make multimedia presentations in their careers.

The Written Word vs. Multimedia

The benefits of reading and writing are unchallenged. Reading requires mental skills that are geared to process and organize ideas, it awakens the imagination, and it is rightly regarded as a higher-order skill, universally desirable for every student of every age in every school system in the world. Similarly, writing, the next step in the process, also develops some highly regarded mental traits, and favors the organized and structured use of language as a means of expression. It is almost every parent's aspiration to see their children become avid readers and good writers.

However, whether we like it or not, multimedia is, to many young people, an initially more attractive medium. Watching a video requires far less mental effort than reading, and less elaborate processing, and, although the resulting mastery of the content is doubtful, more information can be relayed in less time in a video. It is also undeniable that images, and especially beautifully produced videos, can be a much more engaging way of capturing the audience's attention. So, with the advent of the fully searchable almost infinite repository of videos on the Internet, it should come as no surprise that more and more multimedia is being consumed. As video production is easier, faster, and more accessible, it makes sense that video is becoming an increasingly common form of expression.

Online video is even gaining ground on traditional TV usage. One of the latest studies available at the time of this writing, the Consumer Media Usage Study for the second quarter of 2012 (Nielsen, 2012), shows that video viewing online represents around one-third of the time spent watching conventional TV. According to the self-supplied YouTube statistics page, current as of February 2013:

- Over 800 million unique users visit YouTube each month.
- Over four billion hours of video are watched each month on YouTube.
- 72 hours of video are uploaded to YouTube every minute.

In Cisco Corporation's "Cisco Visual Networking Index: Forecast and Methodology, 2011–2016" (2012), experts forecast that Internet video traffic will be 55 percent of all Internet traffic in 2016. There is a growing trend to consume more multimedia to the detriment of every other form of communication.

What are the overall implications of this trend for schools? The impact is far reaching and complex, but there are two issues that clearly stand out. One is the need to reinforce reading and writing skills throughout the normal school curriculum, so as to ensure that students get enough exposure to these still very relevant skills that may not be developed outside of school to the same extent that they used to be when students would read books for entertainment of their own accord. The good news is that most school programs already do a good job of fostering literacy and spending a good number of hours on that part of the curriculum.

The second, much more challenging implication for schools is the need to systematically and scientifically address how to consume and produce multimedia, with an emphasis on presentations and video. There are two sides to this challenge: students need to learn how to decode, analyze, and comprehend multimedia expression so that they can become critical consumers of the media, and they also need to learn how to transmit ideas, thoughts, and concepts through images, sounds, and video.

Before moving into some specific strategies to address the challenge, it is important to clear away the preconception that multimedia, and video production specifically, is a second-class medium of expression. Although it can be difficult to understand and process educational content delivered through multimedia, and it can be argued that the mental processes involved are not so elaborate and rich as those used when decoding text, video, when analyzed extensively, may even contain more subtleties and nuances than written expression. Educators should not disdain multimedia or shrug off their students' multimedia consumption as being almost like vices or as being unproductive in terms of their learning.

Video Comprehension

I often do an experiment with students and adults that illustrates the need to specifically include multimedia decoding within the curriculum. I have found a series of three-minute videos on YouTube that use a variety of techniques to dupe viewers into believing they are reliable and objective. Which videos you use for the example is not important, as long as your choices are masterpieces of viewer manipulation.

In my little experiment, I tell my audience that I will show them some videos and that they need to watch them in silence, to replicate the way people usually watch Internet videos—by themselves. The videos are about the future: the possible effects of technology and how we can expect technology to impact our lives as we move into the future.

Once this sequence of three short videos is run, I ask the audience just two questions. The first one is what they think the message of the videos is, and they all respond that the videos indicate that technology will have an undesirable effect on the future: that the future looks quite bleak and that technological innovations will do more harm than good. Then I ask them the million-dollar question: "Do you think the video is more or less reliable, objective, and well-balanced?" In most cases, even though they know it must be a trick question, they acknowledge that they would say that the videos seem quite objective, especially if I hadn't put them on their guard.

After that, I walk them through some of the techniques used in the videos to convey this feeling that they can be trusted:

- Many different voices in the background read out the various statements about the future that are included as the text of the videos. It is obvious to the viewer that the voices include different genders, ethnicities, ages, and, in some cases, even computer-altered voices, in an attempt to imply that if so many different people are pronouncing the statements, they are generally valid. When I ask my audience how they would feel if just one person were relaying the information, the answer is always that they would be more doubtful and suspicious if the same person were to read throughout the whole video. Further analysis even shows that the use of specific ethnicities and ages with certain phrases that are uttered during the video is intentional.

- The pretended "balanced" messages that include references to a not-so-bad future are invariably done with background images that are either explicitly negative, or that place the viewer in a negative mood by including dark shapes and colors that portray a sense of doom.

• Outrageous and unsubstantiated claims about the future are placed immediately alongside pretended "projections" that have already happened; for example, some biased statement regarding the likely effects of a future technology precedes a supposed forecast that describes smart phones as if they were a thing of the future, in an attempt to validate the previous statement by suggesting that some of the things that they foresaw as future developments are happening already.

• There are too many images flowing throughout the video in very rapid succession, so the viewer doesn't have enough time to consciously process the information that is received. Many of the textual references that are spoken in the video are also very fast paced, so that the viewer does not have time to verify whether the particular statement is substantiated or not.

• Out-of-context images accompany the text in order to impose a very graphic impression on the viewer. For example, bombs and explosions accompany statements about technological development.

After alerting my audience about the techniques utilized throughout the videos, we watch a rerun, and I ask them to stop me when they detect any of these techniques. This step-by-step analysis of the videos yields multiple inaccuracies, contradictions, and false claims mixed in with the techniques used to lead the viewer to believe that the videos are scientifically rigorously produced. I finally ask the audience whether they think they would have detected any of these attempts at misdirection if they had viewed the clips in the privacy of their homes, casually, while simultaneously doing something else, as is often the case. The answer is that in normal consumption of videos they would not have detected most of what goes on within them had they not been alerted and paid more attention.

The point of the exercise is to impress upon the participants the idea that we require a greater degree of critical analysis of multimedia, for the simple reason that it is far easier to fool us by means of a video than through the written word. Another question I ask the viewers is whether they would have been more skeptical had they read all the statements instead of watching the video, and they answer that reading the same stuff would have raised immediate suspicions as to the accuracy of most of what was said.

It is a good illustration of the fact that we need to include in the curriculum learning opportunities that specifically deal with video comprehension, analysis of multimedia, the coding of multimedia, and so on. It's great that we devote so many hours to reading comprehension, but we should also include opportunities to learn the skill of decoding multimedia, and we should grant multimedia comprehension the same pedagogical status as we do reading comprehension, especially since multimedia is a far easier way to surreptitiously lead people into believing things.

Surprisingly, there is very little in the way of exercises and resources to assist teachers in helping students learn video comprehension. However, even though the road needs to be made by our own footsteps, there is quite a lot that we can accomplish by following some common-sense simple steps:

- **Train viewers to disassociate images from text.** Even though developing critical insights is akin to "lost innocence" in that the knowledge gained through it cannot be unlearned and may forever change the viewer's take on videos, being aware simultaneously about images and text and trying to see them separately is a good primer for detecting related inconsistencies or inaccuracies.

- **Watch out for unsubstantiated statements.** Like we would do when reading text on the Internet, we need to watch very carefully for anything that is included in videos for which there is no reference. In the same way that we would expect a footnote referencing claims in a text, the speaker in a video should also find a way to include the source of any claim—statistical information, for example.

- **Read between the lines.** The dominance of the written word in our society is self-evident in the fact that there isn't even a saying to describe the process of inference when decoding multimedia—that is, how to try to understand the implications of whatever is being shown on screen beyond the obvious. Perhaps "see between the frames?" Just as we train students to find the hidden meaning of text by interpreting, for instance, the author's choice of language, and how the words and metaphors are used to imply certain meaning, we must help students develop that skill when analyzing images, sounds, and video as well.

- **Keep a detached perspective.** In general, it always serves the viewer well to maintain a somewhat distant perspective, and to perform reflective analysis on anything that they see. Being sure to not take whatever is being presented at face value may sound a little bit cynical, but it is an essential quality in the 21st century, when the barriers to publication are at an all-time low and anybody with a webcam can put a video on the Internet and profess knowledge of any topic.

Digital Manipulation of Images

A similar challenge has to do with digital manipulation of images by the media. For a long time already, ever since photo retouching programs became available, the media have been sorely tempted to alter photos digitally in ways that help them convey whatever particular message they want to put across.

Some of the infamous cases are very well known, most notably the 1994 cover of *Time* magazine featuring a mug shot of O. J. Simpson that was darkened so that he would appear more menacing, or the photograph taken from the twin towers supposedly as one of the airplanes is about to hit it showing a tourist on the observation deck.

Digital image forensics is a relatively new discipline that deals with the detection of images that have been tampered with digitally. Being able to detect alterations in a photograph is a bit technical in the nature of the task, but students should at least be made aware through systematic learning processes of the possibility of photographs being retouched to show a different reality, and should have some basic notions about how to detect whether images have been changed or not.

Producing Multimedia

Perhaps even more challenging than helping students become critical consumers of multimedia is the task of helping them learn to express themselves through images, sounds, and video. Generating multimedia is a fairly new discipline and one that requires a certain degree of specificity; namely, knowledge of graphic design. We have probably all gone through the humbling experience of painstakingly attempting to develop a graphic document, whether it be a presentation, Web page, brochure, etc.—anything that involves certain graphic skills—and then witnessing a true professional who knows not only the techniques and the tools but also the artistic principles to do it much better than us seemingly effortlessly.

Graphic design should be addressed explicitly and learned as part of the formal instructional program of any school. This entails some hard decisions about prioritizing subject matter, as the curriculum is designed; probably the inclusion of design subjects would be to the detriment of some other subjects, but nothing is more important in this time than to give our students the mechanisms and the tools to express themselves through multimedia.

In most school systems, the "research paper" paradigm is still dominant as the most sophisticated expression of knowledge to be achieved by students upon graduation. However, although this experience can still be very valuable, designing a multimedia presentation to a similar level of proficiency is equally important, mostly for the reason that outside academia, most functioning adults will have to produce many more presentations than papers.

We cannot effectively help our students learn what we ourselves don't know, don't care about, or don't think is important. The first step toward guiding our students in the production of multimedia is to be aware of the extreme importance that students learn this skill in the context of school. Subsequently, teachers will need to learn some of the basics of graphic design and how to operate state-of-the-art software to produce multimedia presentations. There are two main reasons for this. One is that teachers should model expressing themselves through multimedia in a way that exemplifies the learning to be acquired by students, and not just by creating cut-and-paste digital recollections of lessons of the past. This passes along a very important lesson: when teachers dare to move out of their comfort zone and try this relatively new mode of expression themselves, they set an example in terms of communication and also in terms of having the confidence to engage in a trial-and-error learning process in which mistakes are not to be penalized, but rather learned from.

The second reason, of at least equal importance, is that every teacher should be versed in principles of graphic design and presentation production so that, when assessments are given to students that include the production of such presentations or videos, the teacher is able to assess them technically in a way that provides the students with relevant feedback not only about the content but also about the way they are trying to express it. It would be unthinkable for a teacher to accept a written test that is full of grammatical and spelling mistakes.

We want to get to the point where teachers would be equally unhappy with a presentation that is full of text, contains very static images, or, in general, is poorly created. We tend to be much more lax when grading multimedia presentations than when grading written work, because we are not knowledgeable enough to feel confident about the feedback that we can give our students, and also because, deep down, we don't recognize the importance of multimedia as an evolving form of expression in the current learning context.

The Ultimate Paradox and the Advent of the E-book

It is rather paradoxical that I am writing a lengthy text advocating for the increased use of multimedia in all contexts. Could all that I have written so far been expressed through a video? Probably yes, but in order to reach the same level of interest (hopefully) generated by the book, the level of production required for the video would have been totally out of my reach.

The fact that I am campaigning for increased multimedia focus in education from within the safety of the written word is, in itself, a testimonial to the fact that text still has an important and prominent place in the learning process. For a book like this one, which consists of an extended discussion on how to give shape to a 21st-century classroom, the text still makes sense, although the ideal form would be a combination of text with dynamic links to videos, Web-based resources, and other highly engaging and interactive content to be accessed directly from the book itself, in a sort of advanced e-book incarnation.

E-books have been around for quite some time and their existence has long threatened the definitive demise of the paper book, which still stubbornly resists, reinventing itself with bookstores that offer new and innovative services and that are largely financed through the selling of e-book devices and the e-books themselves. There are two reasons why e-books have not definitively swept paper books from the learning game. One is technical. Newer e-book devices that almost double as tablet computers deliver truly interactive electronic books that contain links and multimedia resources, thus really enhancing the reading experience. The problem is that as of yet these devices are still expensive, and their battery life is counted in hours, whereas first-generation e-readers can operate for days without being recharged.

The second reason is much more prosaic. For marketing reasons, and I guess also partly so as to still make paper books feasible, e-books cost only 30 or 40 percent less than their physical counterparts. Because they don't need to be printed and there are no distribution costs, e-books could ultimately end up being priced at a small fraction of the cost of paper books. When that ultimately happens, the very low cost and the irresistible lure of having the book delivered within seconds might signify the dreaded death of the conventional book. Perhaps a good business opportunity would be to patent a fragrance of paper to spray on e-book readers for those who would long for the smell of paper books.

Jokes aside, multimedia e-books are definitely the future of learning, with increasingly more sophisticated degrees of interactivity. Video, images, sound, and text will all form part of the same portfolio, with links to online resources that are dynamically updated along with the content of the book itself, which would be kept current via software that downloads updates. It is interesting to note that this is still in the future for marketing reasons, not because the technology is not mature. Any tablet or smart phone user could be enjoying such books right now for a fraction of the cost they now pay for either electronic books or paper books.

An emphasis on learning multimedia is one of the most urgent needs for change in the school system, because the growth of multimedia expression is unstoppable.

CHAPTER TEN

Games

In the 1986 Disney movie *Matilda*, the archetypically retrograde headmistress of the school, Mrs. Trunchbull, writes something on the blackboard that seems, in a way, to express some of the darker feelings of many teachers, and that resonates deeply with most viewers' school experience: "If you are having fun, you are not learning."

Despite what all learners know intuitively so well, it is almost paradoxical that, yes, in effect, fun and learning have become contradictory in the formal school setting. Mrs. Trunchbull's statement feels so true: our finely honed instincts as educators almost invariably get restless when there is fun, laughter, and enjoyment in the classroom setting. It is as if, even though we know that fun and engagement are conducive to learning, we are indulging in some sort of guilty pleasure by having fun while learning. Here is an acid test for your feelings regarding fun and learning: If you are teaching and have a moment of unrestrained enjoyment in the classroom, would you want the principal to walk in just then? And if an administrator was to conduct an impromptu observation in a class where your students are having fun in the service of learning, would you be worried that your school leader would think that there is too much levity and a lack of rigor in your classroom environment?

What we know deep within holds true: fun and learning are intimately associated, and, as our own experience can attest, significant learning occurs when we are enjoying the experience. Neurologist Judy Willis, one of the most prominent voices in neurodevelopmental research applied to education, makes an unequivocal reference to the benefits of engaging in fun while learning in her book *Research-Based*

Strategies to Ignite Student Learning: Insights from a Neurologist and Classroom Teacher (2006):

> The truth is that when joy and comfort are scrubbed from the classroom and replaced with homogeneity, and when spontaneity is replaced with conformity, students' brains are distanced from effective information processing and long-term memory storage. The highest-level executive thinking, making of connections, and "aha" moments are more likely to occur in an atmosphere of "exuberant discovery," where students of all ages retain that kindergarten enthusiasm of embracing each day with the joy of learning.

Once we get the preconception that fun and learning are mutually exclusive out of the way and acknowledge that fun and engagement are desired objectives in the 21st-century classroom, one important protagonist in the lives of many adolescents becomes an enticing option: gaming.

Gaming should be one of the main and most important activities in the 21st-century classroom. It needs to become the one dominant and salient feature of the new pedagogy, and students should spend more time doing it, even in the sacrosanct environment of the formal school setting.

Of course, games in the learning environment should have learning as a major objective. Games that are specifically designed with learning objectives in mind, that make use of some of the attractive characteristics of play in order to make the learning experience more fun, and that have solid educational content and prioritize learning above all are valuable learning tools.

Elements of a Game-Based Pedagogy

If we break down some of the salient characteristics of a game-based pedagogy, we can immediately see why it can be hailed as the most effective implementation of some of the principles of 21st-century learning. Some of these characteristics are:

High levels of engagement. Even if we disregard the formal research that validates the idea that learning and fun are intimately associated, engagement is a highly desired trait in any learning activity. Educators strive to cross the chasm to students' attention spans and engage their interest; most educators will gladly sign off on anything else as long as engagement is achieved. We all know from our teaching experience that when students are connected there is a much higher chance of significant learning occurring. For the simple reason that they are fun and attractive, games provide an environment where students are instantly engaged, so one of the major prerequisites for learning is almost guaranteed when students play learning games.

Real-time relevant feedback. It is widely accepted that one of the major principles of successful assessment is that students receive relevant feedback that informs their learning such that they can apply that feedback to improve their learning experience. Instantaneous feedback is essential to the gaming experience, since the gamer receives real-time information about whether the objectives in the game are being met or not in the form of the fateful "game over" or loss of lives within the game. Feedback is not only fast, but also well substantiated. In very graphic form, the person playing the games learns why they have not been able to progress any further.

Acceptance of mistakes as part of the learning process. In a keynote address delivered at a conference in 2007, Douglas Reeves expressed wonderfully how the video game environment not only does not stigmatize mistakes but also encourages students to learn from their errors. He pointed out that while playing a game, when students fail, most often, their character literally gets killed. Even so, instead of becoming frustrated, declaring that "it's not fair," and giving up, as they often do when they receive a test with a bad grade scribbled over it in offensive red ink, they keep on trying, learning from their mistakes until they can overcome the obstacle. This particular aspect of the learning experience associated with gaming is perhaps the most valuable of all, and one that is almost exclusive to using games for learning. Anybody who has spent a considerable amount of time in the classroom would be hard pressed to come up with a similarly challenging and yet encouraging process that compels students to persist after failing, not get frustrated by their mistakes, and keep on trying until they get it right. More and more voices have been raised in recent years alerting us about the value of making mistakes, about grit and determination being among the most important characteristics for student success, and about how many studies prove that people who are most successful in life are the ones who can recover from mistakes. There is nothing like the interactive gaming experience to provide a safe environment where students can learn from their mistakes.

Collaboration. Many games, even if they are fiercely competitive, which also acts as an interesting element of the motivation factor for students, are played collaboratively, in teams, so that learning objectives have to be accomplished by teams of players who divide themselves up according to the roles and objectives of the game in order to cooperate toward successful completion of the stages. Even though multiplayer games are mostly based on competition, specifically designed educational games can build upon their characteristics to encourage collaboration. Games such as Minecraft, or even the much more dubious first-person shooters like Call of Duty, allow for the creation of impromptu partnerships between gamers who have just met on the Internet and are exchanging tips and hints and working together toward common objectives online. The same principle applied to educational learning can become a very powerful catalyst for collaboration.

Practical, hands-on learning. There is a well-known adage in education: students remember some of what they read, and only part of what they hear, but they remember everything they do. It is a universally accepted fact that hands-on activities that are realistic in their focus on real-life problems can be indelible learning experiences, as the interactive and practical nature of the work presents students with challenges that need to be solved by pulling together knowledge in a way that results in immediate and visible effects. By their very nature, especially if the level of realism of the game is quite high, games provide a hands-on environment where players have to actually do stuff, and interacting in the gaming environment with objects and characters is an integral part of the experience. Replicating that immersive learning environment with a high degree of fidelity in educational games can develop skills through practical interactions that otherwise would take much longer to perfect.

Increasing levels of complexity. One of the most attractive and relevant characteristics of games for the education environment is that, as students progress in the games, they are presented with increasing levels of complexity through different levels and stages that become progressively more challenging. Games are carefully designed so that each new stage in the game is hard enough that the gamer retains engagement, but not so difficult that they may become frustrated or turned off and stop playing. This setup of progressing into increasing levels of difficulty is a dream come true for any educator, a long-sought scenario that challenges students to develop their skills and learning, but that is gentle enough not to overburden them with tasks that are impossible or frustrate them.

Independent learning/learning from peers. There are times when gamers hit a roadblock and they cannot progress any further in the game. Anybody who has played a video game can recall that familiar feeling of trying everything there is and still failing to resolve a situation, or being baffled because we missed some seemingly unimportant clue along the way and now we can't progress. What do young people do when facing such an obstacle? They definitely do not raise their hands and ask the teacher to assist them in making progress in the game, partly because it is not their natural way to get around these problems, and partly because they know that, more often than not, the adult in the room would not have the answer. What they do is to turn to online forums or look for YouTube videos where they can get walk-throughs, tips, and hints, or even dedicated tutorials on how to get through a certain stage in the game. This fosters habits of independent learning, in that the students are trying to overcome difficulties on their own without the recourse of adult intervention, and also encourages them to make good use of peer-to-peer learning by going first and foremost to other users who have successfully completed the stage. When students are playing in the classroom environment, we often hear calls for help, asking the most proficient gamers for hints or tips on how to progress beyond a certain stage, thus benefiting both the learner and the person dispensing the help, who validates their self-esteem as masters in the game, and affirms their knowledge by teaching it. We would be hard pressed to find an environment in which students can really feel like, and actually be, active contributors to the knowledge society.

Customization. Another feature of video games that is very much in line with the 21st-century pedagogy is that, in general, games can provide for a somewhat customized experience. Whenever a player starts a game, they have to select an avatar, or character, that represents them, and in many cases they can choose some of the defining characteristics of that computer impersonation of themselves. Then, as the game progresses, it is quite frequent that the reward obtained by the gamer for completing stages is some sort of higher degree of customization for the character, or a greater arsenal to increase the capabilities, skill sets, and tools available to the player. More sophisticated games also allow the player to choose from different scenarios and variations on the type of game, including the level of difficulty. This allows for a truly customized experience, and future educational games will no doubt also incorporate adaptive technologies to detect and cater to the learning style of the player, ensuring that progress can be consistent.

Individual and self-paced. We recognize that the needs of individual students vary, and that the learning experience should cater to each learning style and ability. Being able to deliver on this promise is dependent on time, and on the fact that it is empirically evident that students do not all learn at the same pace. This poses some logistics issues in the classroom, especially when it comes to oral explanations that are shared by the whole class, deadlines for assignments, and dates for assessments. One of the most outdated characteristics of the old school model is that learning needs to occur by a specified time and that all students should literally be on the same page. The gaming experience, since it is, by definition, one that students can undertake in their own time, provides for self-pacing of the learning experience, and how long it takes for a gamer to master the game and make progress and thus achieve the learning objectives has no bearing on the success of the player in the end. Progress in a game will equate to learning, and it truly doesn't matter if one student has had to spend more hours playing the game than another one, as long as the learning objectives are met. Attenuating the effect of the time pressure on the learning process can be a great relief for many of the students who find themselves somewhat left behind in the normal environment of oral explanations and collectively timed assignments.

Metacognition. One of the interesting spinoffs of using games in the learning context is that students are able to reflect much better on their learning experience in a game format than if they go through conventional learning. The highly interactive and engaging nature of the gaming experience makes students very aware of the extent and limitations of their own learning. I have done countless interviews with students after they played educational games, and almost every time I have asked them to reflect on the experience. In most cases, they are highly critical of the limitations of the game—how the pretended realism can include some gross oversimplifications of reality— and they are quite conscious of how much more they need to learn in order to master the topic the game covers. This is achieved through the game environment, which usually attempts to replicate a real-life situation that students can easily relate to their own everyday experience. This metacognitive benefit of games is often overlooked, but it does constitute a very relevant and important characteristic of the game-based pedagogy, since reflection and awareness of one's own learning is a survival skill in the quest for lifelong learning.

Whenever we refer to games in the classroom, it seems like some sort of far-fetched proposition that may be hard to visualize. The kind of three-dimensional, immersive, highly realistic games that we are talking about exist in real life—it's just that their focus is not on learning. The most popular video games have high levels of interaction and breathtaking graphics that are almost indistinguishable from video, and they foster engagement levels that far surpass educators' wildest dreams. If we could have such games for historical simulations, three-dimensional renderings of the human body, science simulations of atomic-level chemistry interactions, online collaborative historical role playing, and so on, we could truly take the learning experience to a completely different new level. If such games were available on a regular basis, they would be the most important conduit for delivering on the promise of 21st-century education.

Educational Games

Unfortunately, even though there has been some good progress on the variety and quantity of educational games that are available for use in classrooms, they as yet are nowhere near the level of fun and interactivity that are the norm in commercial games. The reason is quite straightforward: developing games of the quality of commercially sold video games requires multimillion-dollar investments whose returns can only be found through massive commercial success. Despite increasing investments in technology, schools are still far from providing a viable market for the mass development of educational games by companies wanting to create fantastic educational games but still make a profit.

However, there are an increasing number of games available, in some cases for free and in other cases for a moderate fee, that can assist learning in the classroom. With the proliferation of tablets and smart phones, one model of games has emerged as the dominant incarnation of games applied to the classroom—app-based games. These are light applications, quick to download and quite inexpensive in their pricing, providing limited interactivity within a generally narrow scope. Despite their lighter nature, app-based games can be quite useful, and certainly help, especially in the lower grades, to engage students in the learning of certain skills and subject areas, but because of their very nature, although they can provide some of the elements outlined in the preceding sections in terms of the interactive gaming experience, their level of usability is quite low, and the fact that there is a certain lack of content depth, number of levels, realism of the experience, and quality of the graphics does not allow for a truly revolutionary experience in terms of game-based learning.

These apps are getting better with time, and as competition becomes fiercer, we can expect their quality to improve, as well as also combining the increasing capabilities of handheld portable devices in terms of processing power, memory, and video processing. Some scaled-down versions of the more hard-core games are starting to appear for tablets, so there is hope that even these mostly online-based games will be able to deliver on the promise of gaming for education.

An Internet search for "educational games" with any added keyword pertaining to the particular subject matter or age level yields surprising results in terms of the quality and quantity of the options available. The games available are probably not at the level of commercial games yet, but there are many very interesting options, and a good number of them are low-cost or free for downloading in the classroom. The game-based pedagogy may not yet be mature enough to be a mainstream implementation in the 21st-century classroom, but it constitutes a viable and interesting option that can be added now to the resources being utilized in the classroom regularly.

Assessing Learning Through Gaming

Finally, an inextricable part of any pedagogy has to do with assessment. Though it sounds challenging, assessing student learning through gaming surprisingly turns out to be probably the easiest of all assessment scenarios related to the 21st-century pedagogy.

There are basically two approaches to game-based assessment. The first one, not to be ruled out, is to try to transpose the conventional assessment framework on the game environment. This would entail creating a rubric, and/or assigning a numeric grade to gauge the progress of students in the game, and, as such, in the learning experience.

The easiest and most straightforward way of assigning a numeric grade and fitting games into the conventional assessment framework is to measure student progress by means of stages and objectives to be completed in the game, whether it be finishing a certain stage or achieving specific milestones in the game, or scoring a certain number of points. Most games that have educational focus also include a log for teachers to look at that keeps a record of the different stages in the progress of students throughout games. Even by conventional parameters, the teacher can also include an end-of-unit assessment to measure learning the traditional way, as a way to validate the gaming experience. Results will be surprisingly positive, even if the learning in itself is not specifically tailored to be measured that way.

The use of game logs yields very interesting insights about the number of hours spent, levels completed, and speed of progress for each student, and provides the teacher with invaluable information about the learning profile of students. We can also expect that more advanced future games based on adaptive technologies would also provide the teacher with interesting information regarding the learning abilities and thought patterns of students as they play the game.

Debriefing

The other, much more interesting approach to evaluating learning through games consists of using debriefing sessions similar to the ones regularly used in high-pressure and high-stakes environments. One of the major criticisms of our generally outdated assessment systems is that, despite increased awareness of the need to transform assessment from summative to formative so as to inform the learning process, by far the most dominant assessment species is the end-of-unit sit-down written test that students have only one chance to pass. With very few exceptions, most experiences in real life allow for second opportunities and learning from mistakes.

Some of the exceptions to this rule, and ones that are particularly interesting because learning in those activities can equate to survival, are test pilots, astronauts, and surgeons. Those are unforgiving, harsh, and high-pressure environments where mistakes can actually cost lives. If we look at how people in those professions are trained, they definitely don't earn their surgeon credentials or astronaut wings by passing sit-down written tests; the real validation of their proficiency is accomplished through realistic simulations. Surgeons first operate on cadavers, and then accompany skilled practitioners in the operating room, slowly gaining mastery by performing progressively more complicated procedures until they are able to operate on their own.

The example of astronauts is even more graphic in the implications for learning. Rightly hailed as one of the most difficult accomplishments of all times, the moon program presented aspiring astronauts with staggering levels of difficulty in having to master spacecraft that were infinitely complex, in a completely harsh and unforgiving environment. Eventually, astronauts learned to become one with the spacecraft and respond with uncanny reflexes to malfunctions and problems by going through endless drills and simulations, many of which resulted in their simulated deaths. The much-maligned devious simulation supervisors conjured up all types of scenarios where astronauts on their spacecraft met an untimely end, and the astronauts were thus led to sobering realizations about the gravity of the situation and the responsibility to not leave anything unchecked, because a mistake could literally cost them their lives.

But the learning was not only achieved through the trial and error process. A very important part of the simulation was the post-mission debriefing, a no-holds-barred session in which the supervisors and the astronauts and mission controllers dissected the recently simulated mission, analyzed mistakes and errors, and took careful notes so as to avoid repeating those same mishaps. Some of the greater successes of the moon program—for example, the decision to go ahead with the first moon landing despite alarms that had sounded in the cockpit—are due to having gone through those simulated scenarios beforehand and knowing the answers ahead of time.

The implications are very profound for our classroom experience, and, when applying educational gaming, it is important not to yield to the temptation of gauging the gaming experience solely through the lens of conventional assessment, but rather to integrate as an important part of the learning process debriefing sessions that take the built-in, self-evident results of the game or simulation as a starting point and walk the group of students who have worked in a collaborative simulation or game through a step-by-step reconstruction of the process, analyzing mistakes and attempting to repeat the drills until the concepts are mastered.

Play On

Of all the skills and characteristics of the 21st-century environment that we have covered, without doubt, gaming is the one that should be encouraged with unrestrained enthusiasm and without reservation. As more sophisticated educational games come onto the market, games in the classroom can combine the best of both worlds—the fun, excitement, and highly engaging interactive experience of video games and the very rich, detailed, customized, immersive content that makes the learning experience very relevant and long lasting.

Even though playing a game with our younger students would probably be a humbling experience, since kids' degree of sophistication about gaming and their lightning-fast motor coordination skills would put us to shame in any game, it would not be a bad idea to try out educational games in our own free time and allow ourselves to indulge in the somewhat guilty pleasure of learning in a fun way. This would allow us not only to feel what out students feel, and put us more at ease with the prospect of learning through gaming, but also to reflect on our own experience in terms of how we can learn through games. Of course, there is no better way to evaluate the effectiveness of a game, in terms of the rigor and relevance of its content, than to try it out ourselves, and we might even learn a thing or two. And, our students will respect us for trying.

CHAPTER ELEVEN

21st-Century Assessment

More has been written in recent years about assessment than about any other topic in education, perhaps because of our well-known obsession as educators with measuring and judging our students, or perhaps because there is an awareness of how outdated our assessment methods are and how much they need to change in order to meet the 21st-century educational challenge.

Perhaps the most flagrant disconnect in this respect is the still-thriving proliferation of standardized assessments that are the measure by which schools are rated in terms of their success. Although it is widely accepted that standardized testing is intrinsically flawed, and even more so in the face of the new knowledge paradigm and the quest for lifelong learning, the impact of standardized tests on schools is still strong and decisive.

At one of Edutopia's blogs, in an entry titled "Reinventing Assessment for the 21st Century," English teacher Andrew Marcinek (2010) summarizes very clearly what the heart of the problem is:

> Today's students are unlike any other students in history; they have access to more information than any generation in history, yet they are underperforming. Wait … what? Underperforming! In the most affluent country on the planet? The numbers are shocking, but they're real. How did this happen in America? One of the reasons this is happening is because of the way we assess our students. Students are residing in a

20th century classroom equipped for the 21st century. Students are taking 19th and 20th century exams in a classroom that has an interactive white board and 1:1 laptop ratio. This is where our problem begins.

It is not my intention to summarize or repeat any of the extensive and in-depth analyses that have been made regarding new assessment methods such as alternative and authentic assessment.

This chapter will cover some ideas and models for 21st-century assessment that can be of general application; that is, not specific to any of the skills or traits, but, rather, to the very particular educational landscape that awaits us. The extensive literature that exists regarding new assessment methods, and most of the ideas that give substance to professional development programs currently being administered regarding assessment transformation, are applicable as long as they adhere to the main principles and drivers of 21st-century education, and if we don't espouse one school of thought as the one and only solution to our assessment issues. Once again, tackling this very important issue of assessment cannot be done with a single-minded focus, but requires an open mindset that is attentive to the evolving needs of the learning landscape.

Principles of 21st-Century Assessment

In order to guide the ensuing discussion of 21st-century assessment and to give substance to the ideas and strategies that will be presented, it is good to start by enunciating the main principles or drivers of 21st-century assessment:

- **Timely feedback that allows progress.** This fundamental principle of formative assessment is based on assessment *for* learning and not *of* learning. Summative assessment passes a definitive judgment at the end of a unit of study and has no bearing on the learning process. It makes sense that 21st-century assessment should include more elements of formative assessment than summative assessment, so that the feedback received by the learners informs them about how the learning process is going, as a way to make decisions that positively impact the learning experience. Relating it to the context of lifelong learning as the ultimate goal of the school system, devising ways by which feedback is as prompt and as relevant as possible is inherent to lifelong learning, since we don't want to discover that we have gone off-track in our own self-guided learning process when we have already invested a lot of hours and energy on it. The absence of a teacher, which is the defining factor in the independent learning process, requires that alternative mechanisms be found so that in the future, as a lifelong learner, feedback is decisive in guiding the learning process.

- **Personalization.** One of the greatest and most impactful changes in the new paradigm is the acceptance that all children should rise to their maximum potential and that it is our responsibility as educators to find the pathways that lead to that. This intrinsically implies that the instructional processes have to be customized, or personalized, to as great an extent as possible, to find the right balance between playing to strengths and improving weaknesses as per each student's abilities and learning style. Assessment, of course, has to match that process, and it would be meaningless to have a personalized curriculum and then assess every child in the same way. There is a quote often attributed to Einstein that expresses this admirably: "Everybody is a genius. But if you judge a fish by its ability to climb a tree, it will live its whole life believing that it is stupid." Based on this idea of trying to find ways to gauge the progress of students based on their accomplishments and not on a one-size-fits-all testing model, 21st-century assessment must find a way that is feasible in terms of the constraints faced in real-life school situations to achieve this important objective of having personalized assessments.

• **Meaningful motivating factors.** If there is one universal truth across school systems all over the world, it is the dominant role that grades have in schools. Whether it is letter grades, or the sometimes unbelievably precise numeric measurements on a 0-to-100 scale, the grade speaks for itself and is not only the implicit and explicit measure of success for a student in school, but also, regretfully, intimately associated with the self-esteem of the learner. The characteristics of a 21st-century system of assessments do not sit well with a heavily weighted numerical grade culture. The origin of numeric grades is in comparing and rating students to see who does best, and, of course, fair competition is rooted in equal conditions for everybody. Even though we know better, we cannot deny that our instincts as educators are finely honed toward giving out grades within a certain pattern, and making sure that top grades are not easy to come by. The whole notion of having all students get top marks would be unthinkable, and synonymous with a teacher who is not demanding or not rigorous enough.

I frequently tell a true story from my teaching practice. In one of the schools I worked at, we had a computer system that recorded every single grade awarded by teachers in a database, and once, I had the idea of trying to tabulate the grades given over a period of six years by teachers in our middle school. The original intent was to track the differences in performance by students who came from different schools, but when I analyzed the data I was surprised by the results. Over a period of six years, even though the students that had passed through the middle school had obviously all been different, and at least a third or more of the teachers had been changed, the distribution of grades from A to F oscillated, in most cases, by less than two percent, and it followed a Gauss curve of sorts. The spread of how grades were awarded in the school was independent of the teachers and of the students, and seemed to follow some sort of magical or mystical pattern that responded to, probably, the politically correct expectation of how many students should do outstandingly, very well, well, acceptably, or very poorly.

The heavily grades-based culture in our school system must change. If intrinsic motivation should be the prevailing factor in getting students to make an effort and go the extra mile in their learning, it cannot be spurred or catalyzed by failing, or getting a good grade. Motivating factors that might make students feel that they are rewarded by their efforts could be publication on the Web, increasing leadership roles in the development of a certain project, and the possibility of presenting the product of their work.

- **Evaluation that is not fixed in time.** Another characteristic of most of the current assessment systems that we need to counteract is the fixed-in-time nature of learning. Within the model that is heavily reliant on summative assessment, it is more important to learn on time than to learn itself. Even though there needs to be some semblance of order so that the class is manageable, the rigidity of most current assessment systems results in students being unable to cope with simultaneous demands, the stereotypical overscheduling of tests, and the inevitable stress of having to comply with so many obligations at the same time in a high-pressure environment. Without completely ruling out the time dimension of work, an assessment system for the 21st century must be much more flexible and should allow for multiple deadlines, with intermediate checks that allow the facilitator to provide feedback about the project. The framework should allow students to progress at different paces and should incorporate helping students manage their learning process as one of the desired skills in our quest for lifelong learning.

• **Environment in which mistakes are not penalized.** Mistakes are part of the learning process, and overcoming and learning from mistakes is not only intrinsic to learning but also builds character and provides students with the skills they need to persevere through grit and determination. However, most assessment systems are universally geared to punish mistakes by assigning low grades, which erodes the self-esteem of students who feel humiliated by low grades or failure. In the 21st-century world where failure is no longer a stigma, and is even considered to be an almost necessary part of any process, teachers should take care to create an environment where students are allowed to fail and feel safe doing so. Intermittent failure is inevitable in the unpredictable, fast-paced, dynamic environment of the 21st century, and learning to spread the risks so that they are manageable and not so impactful is a life skill that should be included prominently within the school system in order to prepare students for the 21st century. Our assessment system must reflect that.

• **Frequent self-assessment.** Another very important characteristic of a 21st-century assessment system is that it should include numerous, frequent, and progressively more intense opportunities for self-assessment. Self-assessment, often shrugged off as just another way for teachers not to have to do so much work grading, constitutes a very important skill in the lifelong learning process, since learning on one's own implies being able to self-evaluate the extent of our needs, determine how far we have progressed, pose questions, and plan our own learning accordingly.

- **Focus on real-life scenarios.** The opportunities to interact with reality have been magnified exponentially by the advent of the Internet; school-based activities that shorten the distance between theory and practice are now possible, and make for more engaging assessments. One of the timeless criticisms of school assessments is that, quite often, they are based on problems or projects that seem quite removed from reality. Nowadays, the possibilities, especially at the high school level, for bridging the gap and working on real-life problems involving true situations that students can help to solve, not only add an important dimension in terms of student interest and motivation, but also provide them with a very valuable real-life experience.

- **Collaboration.** An explicit important characteristic of 21st-century assessment is that collaboration should be the norm and not the exception, and assessment should not just be evaluation of the individual contributions but also of the collective performance of the team and of how well the team has collaborated.

These defining elements of 21st-century assessment, while not intended as an exhaustive list, are somewhat definitive in that they address the main principles and drivers of 21st-century education. The ensuing sections analyze how to activate 21st-century skills by means of assessment in ways that are applicable to current methods of assessment as well.

Assessing Lifelong Learning

How can we possibly assess lifelong learning—the primary objective of our school system? Our quest for lifelong learning can basically be broken down into two major areas: acquiring the skills for independent learning and developing the genuine desire and motivation to learn for life.

How do we assess independent learning skills? The independent learning process basically amounts to students acquiring study and research habits that are systematic and that they can pursue on their own, so that, when they finish the formal school setting, they will be able to learn on their own. Evaluating whether students are able to master tasks associated with independent learning will consist of making sure that they can, without guidance:

- Search for information.
- Process the data obtained and narrow it down in order to refine and streamline the search process.
- Distinguish the relevant sources and extract valuable information from them, then utilize the information to solve a problem or create a project.

In the breakdown of the skills lies the key of what exactly to assess. Assessing independent learning entails including, in whatever existing rubrics are utilized for classroom assessment, components related to independent learning skills; that is, whether students are able to look for information on their own, process it, etc. We cannot expect students to learn these skills spontaneously, and cross-curricular processes should be in place to ensure that the skills are required progressively and with varying levels of difficulty throughout their school life.

At various levels throughout the years, and with increasing complexity as they grow up, a summative task in that respect would involve presenting students with a certain study topic or general problem and asking them to conduct research, identify the most relevant and important issues within the topic, and apply, without the guidance of adults, their newly acquired knowledge to collaboratively solving a problem or creating a project.

The other dimension of lifelong learning—fostering a genuine desire and motivation to learn—is inherently much more elusive in that it does not lend itself well to evaluation and even less to measurement. However, that does not mean that it should not be assessed. A positive way to include it within the formal assessment process is by sending reports to parents that include observable habits in students, such as how much interest they exhibit in classroom topics, whether they spontaneously look for information on the Internet, how they respond when exposed to videos or other prompts that should trigger curiosity, and so on. Assessments of motivation should be more qualitative than quantitative. But, in order to have students acquire the habit of going to the Internet to search as soon as they have any doubts or they are curious about anything, it needs to be ingrained deeply into them from a very early age that it is a desirable thing to do, and, as with any character trait, consistent exposure to the process and good examples are the only pedagogy that pays off.

Self-Assessment and Designing Assessment Instruments

Self-assessment is a very important characteristic of 21st-century assessment. A close relative to self-assessment is students designing their own assessment instruments, which will then be combined or remixed to constitute the class assessment. A strategy that I have used extensively and that works quite well is to have students come up with not the answers but the questions relevant to the unit, and assignments that relate to those questions. This higher-order skill involves analyzing the topic sufficiently in depth to determine what is important, and subsequently going one step further by prioritizing what somebody should demonstrate in order to accomplish mastery in whatever learning objective is formulated and then actually writing the rubric.

The final assessment administered to the class can consist of the best student-submitted questions and exercises, and within the open sharing environment, if students go to the trouble of reading everything the other students have submitted and trying to learn the answers, they are entitled to top marks.

If we want to engage in even further metacognitive processes, we can involve the students in collaboratively designing a rubric for the assessment, using a typepad, for example, to work together in setting assessment criteria that describe work that is exemplary, very good, good, acceptable, and badly in need of improvement. Even though it cannot be done all the time, closing the circle fully would entail the students correcting assessments from their peers and engaging in collaborative discussions about answers to the assignments, all the time applying the rubrics that they designed themselves.

The teacher is seemingly rendered superfluous in this scenario, but this process actually frees the adult to engage in personal interactions and customize feedback to students, which otherwise would be much more difficult.

Grading Assessments Electronically

One very simple way to make good on many of the promises of 21st-century education and modernize assessment so that it can cater to some of the traits of 21st-century learning is to have students submit assessments electronically, for example via blog posts, as e-mail attachments, via cloud-based document storage and sharing, or through any other electronic form that the teacher can see, make comments and suggestions on, and return for successive iterations until the students get them to satisfaction.

This not only eliminates the dreaded and cumbersome piles of paper that typically are associated with the teacher caricature, but also allows the teacher to make corrections and suggestions without the need to destroy the original, and the student to produce a finished piece of work with no traces of the intermediate process, as one possible way to enforce the idea that mistakes should not be stigmatized.

The electronic medium is more susceptible to plagiarism than traditional hard-copy assignments, since the possible copying and pasting of content is almost undetectable other than by means such as online services that check for plagiarism. But assessments should be designed in such a way that students cannot just paste content from Wikipedia or another source to complete them, and should demand that they utilize higher-order skills that cannot be easily borrowed from another person.

E-portfolios

In order to break away from monotonous text-based assessments and also take assessment to the next level in terms of encompassing many 21st-century skills, e-portfolios can truly deliver an enriched assessment platform that allows students to be evaluated in a context that is more in line with the 21st-century environment.

E-portfolios basically consist of a combination of text, images, sounds, and videos, with or without a sequence, that reflect and document the learning process in a way that can be sequentially planned or nonlinear. One of the great advantages of e-portfolios and using video and photographs is that the process itself can be documented, and not just the learning outcome, and that it provides an easy and fast medium for student interaction.

There are some distinct advantages to using e-portfolios that can be related to the development of a 21st-century classroom. Some of the suggested uses of e-portfolios and their correlation to 21st-century skills are:

- Including, as part of the learning and assessment process, time for students to record a very short audio snippet with their own assessment of how the project is going. Students can be asked to record their own assessment of the progress of the project by a short audio clip, so that the objective of assessing the learning process is met, and allowing them little time so that they don't enter into politically correct mode. The audio clip should be kept very short so that it forces the synthesizing process and allows for more candid responses.

- Cross evaluation of projects. Again, the ease of use and immediacy of video and sound can provide a very interesting opportunity for students to do evaluations of each other's projects as they go along. A mandatory stage in the development of an assigned project e-portfolio could be that students from other groups need to see the project and give their peers their substantiated, educated opinion about how the project is going, thus establishing a critique system that could be based on a rubric for better objectivity.

- Different roles within the group. The e-portfolio effectively supplies multiple opportunities for different collaborative roles to be acquired within the group, most prominently featuring that of documenter, the person on the team who will be in charge of creating the portfolio and documenting the different stages in the development of the project.

- Peer assessment. One very convenient feature of e-portfolios is that they are very easily reviewed. Looking at a series of photographs, and listening to some short audio clips and/or brief videos can be accomplished much faster than having to read a lengthy piece of text, and, as such, they can quite easily be evaluated by the teacher, by peers, and by the authors themselves.

• Self-direction. One possibility when assigning e-portfolios is not to prescribe exactly what should be included in the project, and to have the students decide which of the wide-ranging sources of material that they could use to demonstrate how well the project has been done are selected and included in the e-portfolio. This goes one step further in terms of skills, since they not only have to do their best work but also reflect on which documents and resources would best display and represent their project. This is clearly a real-life skill, since adults often have to build portfolios to represent their career accomplishments.

E-portfolios provide a myriad of opportunities to assess 21st-century skills, as, by definition, digital literacy and the effective use of technology are essential to their effective development. They may be quite challenging for teachers, since they imply a quite different model of assessment and new criteria and rubrics will need to be developed to deal with them, and also because they require an intensive use of technology, which, at least as of now, is somewhat outside many educators' comfort zones.

Assessing Readiness for New Ideas

Even though it may be regarded as one more catchphrase to populate the already cluttered educational jargon graveyard, it is true that one of the important tenets of 21st-century education is the ability to unlearn and relearn. The current environment of dynamic change requires an unprecedented level of openness to new ideas and methods. A statement often attributed to Alvin Toffler is quoted often enough that it has become almost an accepted mantra for 21st-century education: "The illiterate of the 21st century will not be those who cannot read and write, but those who cannot learn, unlearn, and relearn."

It is frequently said that one of the main problems that the older generation faces in the 21st century is that we are often closed to new ideas and deeply rooted in the old methods and the old way of doing things. School, if it is to reflect real life and prepare students for the current and future world, should foster a mindset that encourages them to truly be open to new ideas, a dimension that is reflected in the "unlearning" process.

If we think about assessing unlearning, we truly enter a borderline scenario that can almost be laughable. In theory, we should be evaluating whether students are able to forget their previous knowledge and learn anew, so one can picture a bizarre assessment rubric in which gauging the level of unlearning would require wrong answers to be valued above correct answers. Levity notwithstanding, it is difficult to come up with an assessment framework that truly caters to the unlearning and relearning process. Even though we cannot truly expect that teachers will come up with ways to assess this frequently and throughout the curriculum, having a certain focus on how students can learn a new method without being conditioned by their previous knowledge can be helpful in cultivating the skill.

For example, students can be trained from an early age onward to learn first one method to solve a problem, and be evaluated on it, and then learn another method, which may be a more efficient or better method. A subsequent evaluation would just focus on the problem itself, and part of the rubric for student success would include selecting the more efficient method to solve the problem.

A New Mindset Regarding Assessment

We need to challenge, gradually and as painlessly as possible, some of our most deeply ingrained assumptions regarding assessment. If anything, the 21st-century environment that requires unequivocal authenticity will automatically reject any attempts by educators to perpetuate the idea that assessment is passing judgment on students based on our own self-image regarding learning. Assessment needs to be transformed from a do-or-die, carrots-and-sticks proposition into an integral part of the learning process that informs and supports the learning.

This idea of assessment as judgment is not intrinsically evil, but it originates from the pre-Internet era in which customization was impossible and the industrial economy required that all graduates from the school system emerge with a certain skill set that would be universally applicable to all future developments in their lives.

Anyone who has spent time in the classroom as a teacher knows that assessment is the one instance where teachers really exercise their power. The moments before a test feature students in their most anxious compliance mode, and the buzz of anticipation before handing out the dreaded exams illustrates the ultimate power of the teacher. Once the papers are collected and the teacher takes them home to read, students are constantly prodding us about whether we have corrected them and how they did, and the moment when we hand back our judgment expressed in that fateful mark at the top of their paper is when students are at their most vulnerable.

If we are to make good on the profoundly humanist improvement in our view of education that stems from the realization that every child can learn and that it is our responsibility to provide them with the means to do it, assessment needs to become part of the service dimension that should be intrinsic to our teaching roles. So almost paradoxically, despite all that we have said and written about the technical nuances of assessment in the 21st century, the most important and profound transformation of assessment for the 21st-century classroom is that it should be regarded as part of the mentoring/facilitating process that aims to get the best out of every one of our students. Within that scenario, there is no room for humiliation, for teachers expressing their displeasure through low grades, or for accepting indifferently students' nonefforts, and there is a great need to genuinely immerse ourselves in this quest for lifelong learning.

If we suspend judgment and accept, for one moment, that generating lifelong learners is the most important overarching goal in the learning process, many of our old or current assessment practices collapse under their own weight. A sense of failure will not engender lifelong learners. Summative assessment as final judgment, with no feedback to inform the learning, will not result in increased levels of intrinsic motivation to learn. Not giving students a second chance will not help them learn from their mistakes. Failing students as a consequence of the dry numeric average without regard for their particular circumstances will not teach them that grit and determination pay off. Demanding the same from all students will not foster a mindset that respects talent and diversity. Being inflexible with deadlines does not pass on the message that learning is the first and foremost objective of what we do.

We need an assessment revolution. But it will not be achieved by just changing our methods. It will require a new mindset and, essentially, a desire to redefine ourselves as learners and no longer omnipotent judges who are detached and disconnected from the learning of our students.

CHAPTER TWELVE

Common Core

For U.S. public schools, at the time of this writing, the Common Core State Standards Initiative is, without a doubt, the most significant curriculum driver for the foreseeable future. Published in 2010, these standards have been adopted by the vast majority of U.S. states for almost immediate implementation.

The two master documents that serve as a sort of "holy grail" for school systems are the Common Core State Standards for English Language Arts and Literacy in History/Social Studies, Science, and Technical Subjects and the Common Core State Standards for Mathematics, both encompassing K–12 education. Because of their widespread acceptance, the Common Core State Standards (CCSS) are, logically, a major influence when making decisions about curriculum and delivery. It is relevant to ask ourselves how they relate to and/or foster the learning of 21st-century skills, and, in that process, how they would help prepare U.S. students for the 21st-century environment.

In order to try to determine how well suited the CCSS are for cultivating the learning of 21st-century skills, there are a couple of things to consider about their nature and scope. To start with, the standards are more about expectations and results than the means to get there, so, even though they are very detailed in describing what students have to attain at the different grade levels, they are not prescriptive, and therefore there is quite a bit of leeway regarding the methods of delivery, which allows for the possibility of deploying 21st-century skills without compromising some of those objectives.

It also needs to be noted that even though the widespread adoption of the standards will place them as the de facto core framework for curriculum design, that framework may be minimal—it may constitute a floor but not necessarily a ceiling. Some of this may change when the next generation assessments are deployed, extending the reach of the Common Core standards to accountability at the state and school levels.

The Common Core and 21st-Century Skills

There are some specific instances where the Common Core standards present opportunities for 21st-century skills to be addressed at the classroom level, and this chapter will present some ideas and suggestions as to how to do so.

When it comes to determining whether or not the Common Core will help to develop the 21st-century classroom, there is good news and bad news, and, unfortunately, the bad news is very bad indeed. Despite the opportunities the Common Core standards will open up for the development of certain 21st-century skills, the CCSS were clearly not designed to foster the learning of 21st-century skills, which seem to have been almost completely absent from the thinking that gave birth to the movement. Even though there are some specific references to technology, multimedia, the Internet, and even 21st-century skills, there is a dismal lack of any real analysis and consideration of the new knowledge paradigm and related implications in the Common Core. The whole notion of fixed standards that are immovable and require years to implement and an even longer period of time to fine-tune and assess is completely contradictory to the whole notion of 21st-century learning.

A quick read of both documents would suffice to see that very little regard is given to differentiation or customization of the curriculum, that most of the standards are rooted in the traditional model of schooling, and that expectations are defined in terms of the old paper-and-pen world.

Some statistics on the ELA Common Core document may shed light on its surprising disregard for 21st-century education, both conceptually and in the skills and contents outlined in the documents. Figure 12.1 is a word cloud that portrays the relative frequency of words in the 20,000-word document.

As you can see, or more to the point, rather, as you can *not* see, you would be hard pressed to find within the cloud any words that make direct or indirect reference to the 21st-century learning environment. More specifically, within the 20,000-word document, the word "multimedia" appears only 17 times, "digital" can be found 26 times, "Internet" seven times, and "Web" just one time.

Even worse, the standards for mathematics practically have no words at all that make any reference to 21st-century skills or to the use of the Internet.

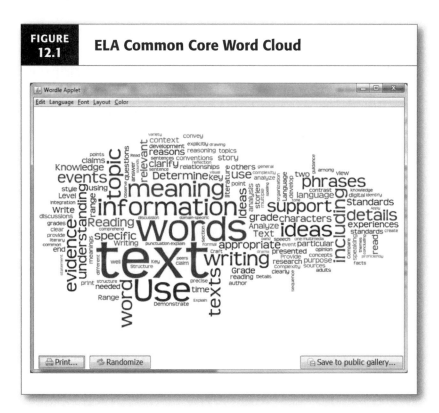

FIGURE 12.1 ELA Common Core Word Cloud

This is not intended to denigrate the efforts that went into developing the standards, or to pass judgment on how good they are for developing literacy and improving the levels of reading and writing. However, what is almost unforgivable is that a document that will, undoubtedly, make such a profound impact on education in terms of the necessary compliance by schools has so blatantly and seemingly deliberately ignored the main drivers and principles of 21st-century education, the importance of which, all in all, transcends the standards when it comes to developing a curriculum for the new learning paradigm. The references to technology that are included in the CCSS are on target and bring out opportunities for developing 21st-century skills, but they are few and far between, and evidently marginal in their focus.

The good news is that the phrasing of the standards themselves, especially in the ELA and literacy standards, is ample enough in its scope that it does allow for opportunities to infuse 21st-century skills into the curriculum by adapting the standards in a way that better lends itself to the fostering of those skills. Even though it will take quite an effort and a certain stretch, the standards can be flexed to accommodate 21st-century skills. If the yet-to-be-unveiled next generation assessment scheme includes adaptive technologies, so much the better.

Direct References to 21st-Century Skills within the ELA Common Core Standards

There are several references to 21st-century skills in the Common Core standards documents (National Governors Association Center for Best Practices, Council of Chief State School Officers, 2010):

- Within the introduction, on page 7, when discussing college and career readiness, there is a direct reference that is very much in line with the principles of 21st-century education. When describing the "portrait of students who meet the standards set out in this document," the very first paragraph reads:

"They demonstrate independence.
Students can, without significant scaffolding, comprehend and evaluate complex texts across a range of types and disciplines, and they can construct effective arguments and convey intricate or multifaceted information. Likewise, students are able independently to discern a speaker's key points, request clarification, and ask relevant questions. They build on others' ideas, articulate their own ideas, and confirm they have been understood. Without prompting, they demonstrate command of standard English and acquire and use a wide-ranging vocabulary. More broadly, they become self-directed learners, effectively seeking out and using resources to assist them, including teachers, peers, and print and digital reference materials."

The last sentence, in particular, targets independent learning as an objective, but the fact that the digital reference materials are left as the last resource mentioned is troubling.

• Within the same page, another part of the "portrait" is directly related to the use of technology and digital media:

*"They use technology and digital media
strategically and capably.*
Students employ technology thoughtfully to enhance their reading, writing, speaking, listening, and language use. They tailor their searches online to acquire useful information efficiently, and they integrate what they learn using technology with what they learn offline. They are familiar with the strengths and limitations of various technological tools and mediums and can select and use those best suited to their communication goals."

The above paragraph is spot on, and constitutes an excellent summarization of what digital media and technology can be used for in the learning process.

- Within the actual standards themselves, the first reference appears in the reading standards for literature for grade 2 students. Under "Integration of Knowledge and Ideas" we can find:

  "Use information gained from the illustrations and words in a print or digital text to demonstrate understanding of its characters, setting, or plot."

This is the first of many references to the digital medium as an alternative source for information. The possibility here is clear: utilize tablets, computers, or other digital media to expose students to reading text and also gaining information from multimedia sources contained in the digital document.

- Another similar reference includes, for grade 5 students, also under "Integration of Knowledge and Ideas":

  "Draw on information from multiple print or digital sources, demonstrating the ability to locate an answer to a question quickly or to solve a problem efficiently."

Again, the digital source is just one more medium, but it provides an opportunity to enrich the implementation of the standards by using technology in a way that is relevant and conducive to lifelong learning.

- The sole occurrence of the word "Web" occurs alongside the previous standards, when grade 4 students are required to:

  "Interpret information presented visually, orally, or quantitatively (e.g., in charts, graphs, diagrams, time lines, animations, or interactive elements on Web pages) and explain how the information contributes to an understanding of the text in which it appears."

• The next pointer can be found within the college and career readiness anchor standards for writing, where within "Production and Distribution of Writing," using the Internet as a medium to publish and collaborate with others is considered:

> "Use technology, including the Internet, to produce and publish writing and to interact and collaborate with others."

This is a worthy goal in itself, and one that presents the teacher with very interesting alternatives to engage their students in real-life interactions on the Internet, publish their products, and learn from their peers.

• In the same section, under "Research to Build and Present Knowledge," students are called out to:

> "Gather relevant information from multiple print and digital sources, assess the credibility and accuracy of each source, and integrate the information while avoiding plagiarism."

Once again, the focus of the standards is spot on, and this one objective within the anchor standards is, in itself, a major objective of the school system, since the activity described requires students to be able to perform effective research without infringing on intellectual property rights and, at the same time, discern the validity and accuracy of the source, which is one of the fundamental building blocks of the 21st-century curriculum.

• Moving into the writing standards, kindergartners, under "Production and Distribution of Writing," are required from a tender age to be able to:

"With guidance and support from adults, explore a variety of digital tools to produce and publish writing, including in collaboration with peers."

This constitutes a welcome opportunity to start utilizing software packages that allow for multimedia creation appropriate to the level of maturity of children at that age. Even though the references refer to writing, it can conceivably be stretched, especially at a very young age, to include multimedia.

• This same standard is repeated for grades 1 and 2, but in grade 4, there is an almost laughably anachronistic requirement for students to "type a minimum of one page in a single sitting," which is extended to two pages for grade 5, and three for grade 6. This may very well be a great example of how the references to new technologies and 21st-century skills almost seem out of place within the general spirit of the document, and constitute only cosmetic inclusions that don't address the real change needed. Even though keyboarding can be a useful skill and is still learned in many schools with excellent results that serve students well in their interaction with digital media, I do not think that a foundational document like the Common Core State Standards should prescribe how many pages need to be typed in grades 4 and 5; this is completely counterintuitive to the 21st-century learning environment. To start with, typing ability is not of sufficient importance to justify its inclusion within the standards. Also, it's possible that in the years to come, keyboarding may very well be a skill of the past, or an alternative for those who are not comfortable with or capable of dictating to the computer. Speech-to-text engines are even available in smart phones these days.

- The evolved standard for grade 8 includes some more-encompassing references that allow the 21st-century-minded teacher to engage in a wide variety of activities related to publishing on the Internet in more sophisticated ways:

  "Use technology, including the Internet, to produce and publish writing and present the relationships between information and ideas efficiently as well as to interact and collaborate with others."

- The writing of the standard for grades 9, 10, 11, and 12 even incorporates collaboration:

  "Use technology, including the Internet, to produce, publish, and update individual or shared writing products in response to ongoing feedback, including new arguments or information."

- In grades 3, 4, and 5, the writing standards also include, with gradually increasing levels of complexity, research activities. The standard for grade 5 reads:

  "Recall relevant information from experiences or gather relevant information from print and digital sources; summarize or paraphrase information in notes and finished work, and provide a list of sources."

Once again, the reference to the digital sources is almost an afterthought. However, we need to grasp this opportunity that directly allows us to start students in grades 3, 4, and 5 in the research process, so as to start developing the badly needed reflexes from a very early age and help them become intuitive and efficient searchers and researchers as they progress in school.

- When introducing the college and career readiness anchor standards for speaking and listening, a passing reference is made to the role of new technologies:

"New technologies have broadened and expanded the role that speaking and listening plays in acquiring and sharing knowledge and have tightened their link to other forms of communication. Digital texts confront students with the potential for continually updated content and dynamically changing combinations of words, graphics, images, hyperlinks, and embedded video and audio."

At the risk of sounding cynical, it is difficult to resist the temptation to take a stab at this somewhat insipid and innocuous reference to new technologies. In particular, the last part of the paragraph seems to reflect a very superficial approach to the potential of the Internet as a catalyst for learning and the new technologies as a medium of expression.

• Within the same introduction, under the heading "Presentation of Knowledge and Ideas," a mention is made of the use of technology and digital media for presentations:

"Make strategic use of digital media and visual displays of data to express information and enhance understanding of presentations."

Again, there seems to be quite a disconnect here. Even though these explicit references open up opportunities for the use of digital presentations and data within the curriculum, in real life, it will be the dominant form of presenting and, thus, of having to apply your skills in terms of speaking. Within this introduction that sets the tone for the standards, the use of digital media is just one more of the forms of expression.

• As a side note within the same section, a comment is made about how the Internet has opened up new possibilities for speaking and listening:

"New technologies have broadened and expanded the role that speaking and listening play in acquiring and sharing knowledge and have tightened their link to other forms of communication. The Internet has accelerated the speed at which connections between speaking, listening, reading, and writing can be made, requiring that students be ready to use these modalities nearly simultaneously. Technology itself is changing quickly, creating a new urgency for students to be adaptable in response to change."

Once again, there is nothing to object to in the statement, but the standards for speaking and listening that follow do not make good on the "new urgency" alluded to in this introduction.

• In the sequence, there are several references to the use of digital sources as one of the ways to find information, in terms of consulting a dictionary and thesaurus for finding the meaning of words.

• The next reference to 21st-century learning occurs within the reading standards for informational text. Within "Integration of Knowledge and Ideas," grade 8 students are required to:

"Evaluate the advantages and disadvantages of using different mediums (e.g., print or digital text, video, multimedia) to present a particular topic or idea."

This constitutes a healthy suggestion, since it calls for a higher-order thinking skill in order to reflect on what information needs to be presented and what the best medium for doing so is. This opens up avenues for teachers to discuss the scope, extent, range, advantages, and disadvantages of the different media, including publication on the Internet or the use of presentation software.

- In the writing standards, under "Research to Build and Present Knowledge," students in grades 6, 7, and 8 must:

> "Gather relevant information from multiple print and digital sources, using search terms effectively; assess the credibility and accuracy of each source; and quote or paraphrase the data and conclusions of others while avoiding plagiarism and following a standard format for citation."

As can be seen, the preceding paragraph describes very adequately what needs to be learned in terms of the research process, and it even includes having students learn how to cite sources. The same paragraph is repeated all the way up to grade 12.

- As part of the speaking and listening standards, under "Presentation of Knowledge and Ideas," students are required to:

> "Make strategic use of digital media (e.g., textual, graphical, audio, visual, and interactive elements) in presentations to enhance understanding of findings, reasoning, and evidence and to add interest."

Even though the focus of the preceding paragraph cannot be argued with, at the risk of nitpicking, one cannot help but wonder how digital media can be used in presentations to enhance understanding and to add interest. The undertone seems to imply that the digital media is just an add-on for spicing up presentations but not necessarily integral to the presentation itself.

- Very similar references to the ones outlined in the previous paragraphs are also made within the subsequent writing standards for literacy in history/social studies, science, and technical subjects.

21st-Century Skills
within the Math Common Core Standards

Without making any judgment on the relevancy and effectiveness of these new standards for mathematics, how the topics are structured and sequenced, and their usefulness in fostering more significant learning in mathematics, it is almost self-evident that they are not a springboard for 21st-century learning.

There is room in the standards to utilize computer software, access interactive math-related Web pages, find online simulations and games, and help students learn some of the elements regarding the handling of information (overabundant data, out-of-range data, etc.), but the use or lack thereof of certain terms speaks for itself.

Within the 40,000 word document:

- The word "Internet" never appears.

- "Web site" appears only once.

- "Digital" is used once in the same sentence as "Web site," and then several times when referring to digital clocks.

- "Multimedia" cannot be found either.

- "Computer" is used first in a paragraph referring to how to help students with disabilities, and within a high school standard when it is mentioned that computer algebra systems can be used alongside calculators and spreadsheets. A similar reference is made in the high school algebra standards shortly afterwards, and within modeling standards. The final appearance of the word "computer" occurs in the introduction of the standards for geometry, with no real application.

It is not my intention to express any opinions regarding how good the standards are from a pedagogical point of view in terms of the learning of mathematical skills, but the above statistics are quite appalling. It is, without doubt, a missed opportunity, since an embedded mindset regarding 21st-century learning for mathematics could have worked wonders in terms of preparing our students and helping our teachers develop the means to acquire the 21st-century skills that math can help catalyze.

A Matter of Focus

Despite the fact that they are clearly not geared toward advancing the cause of 21st-century learning, the Common Core standards still provide plenty of opportunities to infuse 21st-century learning activities within the curriculum.

Judging from the current obsession with the Common Core, the greater risk in terms of the impact on education of the standards lies not in the actual standards themselves, but, rather, in the collective frenzy to single-mindedly focus on the implementation of the Common Core, which seems to leave room for nothing else in terms of pedagogical considerations as we look into the future. It appears that, at a time when the professional development needs of teachers in general are so difficult to define and a new model needs to be created, the advent of the Common Core provided a much-longed-for opportunity to re-embrace a one-size-fits-all blanket program that channels professional learning energies in a single direction.

With the highly probable accountability link to standardized testing that awaits the implementation of the standards, it will be hard for administrators and teachers to distance themselves from the Common Core mania and do what is required in terms of developing a 21st-century learning mindset—that is, develop and implement pilot projects, take risks, and move away from the comfort zone of narrowly defined outcomes and fixed expectations. If that happens, the Common Core may become one more well-intentioned educational policy experiment that will perpetuate the old education model and not take us into the future.

CHAPTER THIRTEEN

A Day in the 21st-Century Classroom

One of the main problems in trying to advance schools toward implementation of a true 21st-century curriculum has to do with the difficulty of conveying to the public at large the need for a totally different school system. Even if we were able to magically align expectations and create a universal vision shared by all teachers and administrators about what 21st-century education could really yield in terms of redefined rules for schools, there would still be a need to bridge the gap between that educational vision and what the parents of children in our schools have grown over the years to think that school should be like.

Current school systems, which in many ways still mirror the kind of school experience that adults have gone through, have failed to capitalize on the many opportunities presented by the recent technological developments and, as such, have reinforced the status quo. As a result, there are no self-evident societal demands for a different type of school, and attempts at designing a new curriculum and pedagogy, on top of the technical hurdles and adaptive challenges to overcome, also have to deal with a certain ingrained skepticism regarding educational innovation.

Even if all stakeholders were to agree with every one of the principles outlined in this book, it would still be difficult to put it all together, and it would be a long-term process. In that context, it is useful to indulge in a visualization exercise about what the school of the future may look like. The following fictional dialogue between two girls is set in the school of the future, when the promises of 21st-century education and emerging technologies finally materialize. There are no outrageous ideas embedded in the fictional account; it is only the consolidation of some incipient developments.

Julie and Amy meet after a long and grueling day at school. They are about to go home.

Julie: Are you done?

Amy: Yes, I think so. I am *so* tired—and it's not even 4 p.m.! I just finished soccer practice.

Julie: I know … we still have a long way to go. At least *I* do—I have to study at home, watch videos, get the projects done. Sometimes I think that they had it easier in the old days, when they just went to school and studied. Can you believe it? They even had a schedule, with something to do at every hour of every day. They practically didn't have to decide anything at all: the teachers told them everything they had to do. Now, we have to take care of *everything*. I am so stressed out.

Amy: My mom tells me they had an agenda—a notebook where they wrote down all they had to do. They even had rules that teachers could not give more than three tests a week. Wouldn't *that* be nice. It's not fair that we need to take care of our assessment ourselves. When she talks about her school days, it seems like another world. Can you imagine the teachers and the school telling you whether you passed or failed, so you didn't have to do anything about evaluating your own learning?

She said it was dreadful, but it seems easy compared to what we have to do.

Julie: Mmm ... Yes. I love my freedom, but sometimes all this business of setting targets and objectives and keeping track of them, ticking off our road maps, managing all these projects we have, I think it was much better in the old days. What I don't understand about all that is how somebody else could tell you whether you learned or not, and say whether you passed or failed. Who would want to not learn? You wouldn't have a future.

Amy: Anyway, talking about the good old days won't do us any good; I have *so* much to do.

Julie: How bad is it?

Amy: Ugh. I don't even know where to start. Listen: first, at 5, I have a teleconference with my international project team—we still haven't gotten through design phase, the guy on our team who documents is lagging behind, we have peer review coming up in 10 days, and we're nowhere near ready. Then, I have to do some virtual tutoring for my community service project.

Julie: What are you doing there?

Amy: It's actually pretty cool: I'm tutoring a group of girls in a school in Pakistan in math. We connect online and we do exercises. I explain things to them, give them assignments and correct them, but today I don't have the level of energy I need for them—I think I'm going to show them a video.

Julie: I signed up to do tech support on the school's online forum. Sometimes I get questions that are *un*believable. You know, I can't understand how some people ask such obvious things, when you can find everything online.

Amy: Then I need to put some hours into playing Ancient Rome online. My campaign isn't going as well as I expected. Our historical accuracy rating is falling off all the time. I have some people on my team who are dragging their feet. And I need to make it to the leaderboard for my college application: I want to major in history, and unless I improve my team's score, I don't stand a chance of getting into the program I want.

Julie: That's rough. I played a few times, but I never made it past the first couple hundred years of the empire.

Amy: And *then*, if I still have time and I'm not dead from spending so many hours on the computer, I have to go to the market fair to interview people from the farms on how to cultivate stuff and all that. I have to do my local cultural portfolio and I don't have enough material. What about you? What kind of day do you have?

Julie: I have quite a lot too. Our geography teacher wants us to find something in Google Earth VR that she hid somewhere in the Andes, and she has this software that allows her to hide something different for each person, so I will probably have to spend hours exploring those mountains.

Amy: I've heard the Andes are very pretty.

Julie: Yeah, sure, but not when you have to study. I'd love to really go there someday, and not have to answer these stupid questions and puzzles to get from one place to the other. Anyway, then I am the designated facilitator for tomorrow's study group and we have some little kids in there, so I'd better get ready for that. I need to preview all the videos. Then there's always something else that I have to do. We are working on this project of a robot to help out people in a nursing home and we are stuck on the artificial intelligence algorithm. Also, I need to update my blog, just in case the instructor looks at it today, and I have to look at my friends' blogs and write comments. You know—the usual stuff.

As they are about to leave the school, Amy's phone vibrates.

Julie: Was that your phone?

Amy: I think so. Let me check. Oh no! I forgot to check in with Mr. Samuelson. He asked me to go to his room so he could give me feedback on my assignment. Sometimes I think I should just turn off the GPS. The rotten thing doesn't let me forget *anything*. (She looks at her phone.) Call Mr. Samuelson. (She aims a forced smile at the phone's screen). Hi, Mr. S. Can I go to your room now? Okay, I'll be there in five. (She puts the phone away.) Oh, how I want to finish this math project!

Julie: Math? But Mr. Samuelson is our music teacher!

Amy: Yeah, but you know how I'm always having trouble with math, and since I love music, I'm learning math through music. It's a great program: I'm learning the algebra stuff through scales and musical composition. It's so much easier that way.

Julie: Don't forget to put on your G-glass. You know we have to wear them at all times in school. If Mr. Samuelson asks you something and you don't have it on....

Amy: (Sighs, puts Google Glass on.) Activate Facebook search ... Mr. Samuelson. (She turns.) Julie, I have to go. I'm going to see what Mr. S is up to on Facebook on my way to his room—might score me a few points with him....

Julie: Good luck; see you tomorrow!

The following day, Julie and Amy meet again as they come into school.

Julie: Hey Amy, how are you?

Amy: I'm good. A little tired, actually. This idea of doing intercultural studies with that school in Australia may have sounded great on paper, but the people who wrote up the plan did not have to do a conference call at 3 a.m. I swear, the next one better be in our time zone.

Julie: You should take a nap today at the cave. I love to escape there and have quiet time to myself whenever I can. Do you have time? I think they're doing submarine ambience today. It's one of my favorites.

Amy: I'm not sure yet, I haven't done my schedule for today. I'm going to meet with my tutor now. I have my leadership course in the morning, and a meeting in the afternoon with my group—we have survival project all day tomorrow.

Julie: I did mine last week; I'm glad I got it over with.

Amy: Was it tough?

Julie: Yes, it was quite a pain. They give us some pretty basic stuff and we had to come up with a design of a structurally resistant habitat. The teachers were all having fun at our expense. It's so hard when you can't consult the Internet or computer or anything! I don't know *why* they do it ... as if we would ever not be able to access the Internet!

Amy: Old people stuff ...

Julie: It still makes more sense than those "imagination" sessions. I can't figure out why they would have us all sit in a room "projecting images in our minds," and then ask us all kinds of weird questions about it. It's *creepy*. I have to run; I have my study group now, and then a design workshop for almost the whole day. When I finish school I am not going to design another thing in my whole life.

Amy: See you at lunch?

Julie: I'd love to, but I have a diagnostic session. I have to update my adaptive profile on the computer for the final exams.

Amy: I have to do mine soon too. I hate it, but our parents had it worse. Did you know they had to do multiple-choice exams with pencil and paper and only learned about the results weeks later? I don't think I could stand it.

Julie: And they all studied the same things! How ridiculous is that? Imagine if you and I did all the same things in school!

Amy: Yeah, um, no thanks. You can just keep your nursing home robot away from me. But, have a great day! Will I see you tonight?

Julie: Yes. It's great that we're on the same team for the virtual reality project. See you!

The Learning Revolution

We are at the cusp of a great learning revolution. The new infinite knowledge paradigm, emerging technologies, and rapidly expanding networking capabilities are all converging toward providing students with unprecedented opportunities to learn more, learn better, and stretch human abilities to previously unheard-of levels.

As educators, we are faced with the formidable challenge of translating that learning revolution to school practice. And it is a task of gargantuan magnitude, because of the very rigid structures and preconceptions about what is right in education, confusing external stimuli, the lack of a clear driver for improvement, and innumerable other constraints that seem to render the attempt almost futile.

And, yet, there is a way. It is always tempting to think of this learning revolution in the conventional terms of a revolution—a sudden and explosive movement that brings forth drastic, dramatic, and rapid change. It is highly unlikely that such an approach would have any chance of success, since the barriers are many and the apparent magnitude and scope of the change needed would likely alienate governments, school authorities, and any other organization capable of leveraging a large-scale impact on education.

The answer is to slowly, subtly, and silently lead a quieter sort of revolution, without fanfare but decisively converting our curriculum into one that encompasses the principles of 21st-century learning so as to gradually gain the mindset shift needed.

In *Start Something That Matters* (2012), Blake Mycoskie, the founder of TOMS, which donates one pair of shoes to children in need for every pair of sandals the firm sells, shares a similar philosophy:

> By starting small, you can work through your story, try out your idea, and test your mettle. There's a Japanese concept known as kaizen, which says that small improvements made every day will lead to massive improvement overall. This idea was made famous in the 1980s by Japanese car manufacturers, who very slowly but surely established a dominant position in the American automobile market by adding small improvements to their vehicles rather than introducing revolutionary innovation. When you keep this concept in mind, reaching big goals seems much less scary.

In our quest to advance the cause of 21st-century education, we can relate to this strategy of small improvements toward very ambitious change. Changing the status quo will require persistence, and being grounded in principles more than in particular methods. After all, this is not a philosophical battle about what is best in pedagogy, but a really heartfelt effort to take advantage of educational abundance to improve the lives of children.

Will we ultimately be successful? It is almost contradictory to the whole notion of 21st-century learning to measure success, so, instead, I would much rather answer through the immortal words of Joseph Addison (1712) in his classic play *Cato*: "'Tis not in mortals to command success; but we'll do more, Sempronius, we'll deserve it."

REFERENCES

Bernard, S. (2010). Neuro myths: Separating fact and fiction in brain-based learning. Retrieved from http://www.edutopia.org/neuroscience-brain-based-learning-myth-busting

Blakemore, C. (2011). Neuroscience: Implications for education and lifelong learning. Retrieved from http://royalsociety.org/policy/projects/brain-waves/

Brookhart, S. (2013, February). Assessing creativity. *Educational Leadership, 70*(5).

Carr, N. (2011). *The shallows: What the Internet is doing to our brains.* New York, NY: Norton.

Cisco Corporation. (2012). Cisco visual networking index: Forecast and methodology, 2012–2017. Retrieved from http://www.cisco.com/en/US/solutions/collateral/ns341/ns525/ns537/ns705/ns827/white_paper_c11-481360_ns827_Networking_Solutions_White_Paper.html

Class. (n.d.). In Online Etymology Dictionary. Retrieved from http://www.etymonline.com/index.php?allowed_in_frame=0&search=class&searchmode=none

Critical Thinking Community, The. (1987). Defining critical thinking. Retrieved from http://www.criticalthinking.org/pages/defining-critical-thinking/410

Cross, J. (2006). *Informal learning: Rediscovering the natural pathways that inspire innovation and performance.* San Francisco, CA: Pfeiffer.

Cuban, L. (1993). Computers meet classroom: Classroom wins. *Teachers College Record, 95*(2), 185–210.

Dweck, C. (2007). *Mindset: The new psychology of success.* New York, NY: Ballantine Books.

Gardner, H. (2006). *Multiple intelligences: New horizons in theory and practice* (2nd ed.). New York, NY: Basic.

Gillmor, D. (2004). The former audience joins the party. Retrieved from http://www.authorama.com/we-the-media-8.html

Goldacre, B. (2008, Feb. 16). Banging your head repeatedly against the brick wall of teachers' stupidity helps increase blood flow to your frontal lobes. *The Guardian.*

Marcinek, A. (2010). Reinventing assessment for the 21st century. Retrieved from http://www.edutopia.org/reinvent-assessment-21st -century

Mistry, P. (2009). *The thrilling potential of SixthSense technology.* Retrieved from http://www.ted.com/talks/pranav_mistry_the _thrilling_potential_of_sixthsense_technology.html

Mitra, S. (2012). *Beyond the hole in the wall: Discover the power of self-organized learning.* TED Books, Kindle Single.

Mycoskie, B. (2012). *Start something that matters.* New York, NY: Spiegel & Grau.

National Governors Association Center for Best Practices & Council of Chief State School Officers. (2010). *Common core state standards.* Washington, DC: Authors.

Nielsen Corporation. (2012, May). Global online consumers and multi-screen media: Today and tomorrow. Retrieved from http://www.nielsen.com/us/en/reports/2012/global-online -consumers-and-multi-screen-media-today-and-tomorr.html

Ravitch, D. (2010). *The death and life of the great American school system: How testing and choice are undermining education.* New York, NY: Basic Books.

Reeves, D. (2007). Keynote address at ESSARP Conference, Rosario, Argentina.

Richardson, W. (2012). *Why school? How education must change when learning and information are everywhere.* TED Books, Kindle Single.

Sahlberg, P. (2011). *Finnish lessons: What can the world learn from educational change in Finland?* New York, NY: Teachers College Press.

Sarkar, C. (2005). Herb Kelleher: The complete interview. Retrieved from http://www.christiansarkar.com/2005/11/herb-kelleher-the -complete-int.htm

Thomas, D., & Seely Brown, J. (2011). *A new culture of learning: Cultivating the imagination for a world of constant change.* CreateSpace.

Trilling, B., & Fadel, C. (2009). *21st century skills: Learning for life in our times.* San Francisco, CA: Jossey-Bass.

Weinberger, D. (2012). *Too big to know: Rethinking knowledge now that the facts aren't the facts, experts are everywhere, and the smartest person in the room is the room.* New York, NY: Basic Books.

Willis, J. (2006). *Research-based strategies to ignite student learning: Insights from a neurologist and classroom teacher.* Alexandria, VA: ASCD.

YouTube. (2013). Statistics. Retrieved from http://www.youtube.com/ yt/press/statistics.html

ABOUT THE AUTHOR

 **Gabriel Rshaid** has been an educator for almost 25 years, having taught various subjects at the elementary and high school levels. For the last 15 years, he has been a K–12 principal in independent schools, while still remaining active in the classroom.

His passions for lifelong learning and for technological developments have taken him on the intellectual journey of thinking about how education fits into the context of the new knowledge era and how the 21st-century scenario of infinite knowledge can impact our lives decisively, which has led him to present in numerous venues on the topics of 21st-century education and the future of learning.

He currently resides in Buenos Aires, Argentina, with his wife, daughter, and son.

INDEX